UNCOMMON VALOR

UNCOMMON VALOR

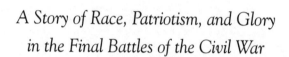

*A Story of Race, Patriotism, and Glory
in the Final Battles of the Civil War*

MELVIN CLAXTON
AND
MARK PULS

WILEY

John Wiley & Sons, Inc.

Published by John Wiley & Sons, Inc., Hoboken, New Jersey
Published simultaneously in Canada

Design and composition by Navta Associates, Inc.

For general information about our other products and services, please contact our Customer Care Department within the United States at (800) 762-2974, outside the United States at (317) 572-3993 or fax (317) 572-4002.

Wiley also publishes its books in a variety of electronic formats. Some content that appears in print may not be available in electronic books. For more information about Wiley products, visit our web site at www.wiley.com.

Library of Congress Cataloging-in-Publication Data

Claxton, Melvin, date.
   Uncommon valor : a story of race, patriotism, and glory in the final battles of the Civil War
/ Melvin Claxton and Mark Puls.
       p. cm.
   Includes bibliographical references and index.
   ISBN-13 978-0-471-46823-3 (cloth)
   ISBN-10 0-471-46823-1 (cloth)
   1. United States—History—Civil War, 1861–1865—Participation, African American.
2. United States—History—Civil War, 1861–1865—Biography. 3. African American soldiers—Biography. 4. Medal of Honor—Biography. 5. United States. Army—African American troops—Biography. 6. United States. Army—African American troops—History—19th century. 7. United States. Army—History—Civil War, 1861–1865. 8. United States—History—Civil War, 1861–1865—Campaigns. I. Puls, Mark, 1963–II. Title.
   E540.N3C58 2006
   973.7'415'0922—dc22

                                                                       2005006842

Printed in the United States of America
10 9 8 7 6 5 4 3 2 1

To my mother, who taught me to read, and my father,
who showed the benefits of being well read

—Melvin Claxton

To my parents, Gerald and Sheron Puls, who gave me
my faith and taught me to love history

—Mark Puls

CONTENTS

A DEBATE OVER CIVIL RIGHTS

A war that can pit brother against brother can also pit a man against his most deeply held beliefs. For Congressman Benjamin Butler, America's tumultuous and bloody civil war had forever altered his views on race in a way he likened to the Apostle Paul's conversion on the road to Damascus. Now with the great debate of the generation, the civil rights of black Americans, still raging a decade after the war seemed to have settled the matter, Butler found himself on the side of a race he once treated with contempt and disregard.

On the floor of the U.S. House of Representatives that January 1874 was a bill that would end discrimination against blacks in public places such as restaurants, hotels, theaters, and restrooms. The bill, which had generated contentious debate, held special significance for Butler, the white general from Massachusetts who once led thousands of blacks into battle in America's bloodiest war.

The bill's passage would be a fulfillment of a promise made

ten years earlier on a little-known battlefield at New Market Heights, near Chaffin's Farm, between Petersburg and Richmond, Virginia. The battle, which few in Congress were even likely to have heard of, had become just a footnote in the annals of the war.

But what happened that day on the rolling hills and grassy knolls was the stuff of legend. Stories of the bravery displayed by black troops were still being told, from church pulpits to inner-city saloons to the remote farms of sharecroppers. In the face of unbelievable terror, laborers, shipping clerks, and simple farmhands had shown unmatched courage, uncommon valor.

Butler recommended fourteen of these black soldiers for the Congressional Medal of Honor for action during the battle of New Market Heights. They had, his recommendation noted, demonstrated courage worthy of the highest honor given to a soldier. The medal bearers represented not only themselves, but the more than 870 black soldiers killed or wounded in the battle. They overcame every kind of doubt and prejudice, disproving widespread predictions that at the first sign of danger they would be found cowards. These men, with little formal military training, enlisted from every walk of life, proved themselves and their race under withering gunfire in the heat of a ferocious battle.

From his office in the Capitol building, Butler could see the hazy figures of men shoveling the streets of Washington, dim silhouettes of gray against the perpetual white of the blizzard that had buried the nation's capital. By the morning of January 6, 1874, the blustery conditions and driving snow had died down and towns throughout the Northeast were digging out. The damage in the storm's wake was extensive. Roads were impassable and telegraph lines snapped under the weight of ice and snow, completely shutting down communications to the region. But Butler suspected that the gallery of the U.S. House of Representatives would be as packed as it had been all week.

Even as he gathered his papers, Butler's thoughts turned to the stormy debate over the past few days. It had run the gamut: ugly, hateful, eloquent, and at times even brilliant. In particular, he recalled with distaste the speech of his old adversary, Alexander Stephens, a representative from Georgia and former vice president of the late Confederate States under President Jefferson Davis.

The often-caricatured Stephens, a peevish little silver-haired man with feeble, deeply wrinkled features and a shrill, piping voice that carried across the floor, railed against the bill as plainly unconstitutional. His physical appearance belied a savvy, calculating politician. Stephens understood the power of images and words, bolstering his position as a legal purist by delivering his speech from behind a formidable wall of law books on his desk near the rear of the House.

Stephens argued that the bill wasn't really about ending discrimination against blacks, but was solely an attempt by some members of Congress to expand their power over individual states. As he concluded his speech to loud applause, he sank slowly into his chair, his eyes fiercely defying opposition.

A small crowd gathered around Stephens's desk as he spoke, and now they waited for a response to the popular congressman. It came from Alonzo Ransier, a black congressman from South Carolina, who wanted the bill to go further and extend equal rights not only to black men, but black women too.

This suggestion brought Congressman John T. Harris of Virginia to his feet. Tiring of the niceties of the debate, Harris immediately began a tirade against the bill. His speech grew more impassioned as he spoke, and his denunciation of the notion of equality climaxed with a challenge. "I defy any man to say that the black man is the equal to the white man," he shouted.

The challenge was met by Ransier himself, who unequivocally stated that he had the courage to say "the black man was equal of the white man."

Harris viciously snapped at him: "You sit down, sir. I am talking to white men and gentlemen, not to you."

There was a moment of awkward silence on the floor, followed by an uproar from delegates and those in the gallery. Another member of the House rose in defense of Ransier, reminding Harris that the black member had the same rights on the floor as he did.

But Harris persisted with his argument. He agreed with Stephens that the bill was not only unconstitutional but that its call for desegregation of schools would lead to the destruction of the existing school system in the South. And that the separate colored and white lunatic and blind asylums in Virginia would be ruined if black and white blind persons were compelled to live together.

Butler recalled the proceedings of the previous two days with a profound sense of sadness. How soon were the lessons of war forgotten. Today was his day to testify, to tell those gathered that he had lived and fought with the black man and had found nothing wanting. He was there that day in late September when the heroes fell. He knew their free-flowing blood represented far more than a garish crimson stain on the bright green of the countryside. They gave their lives to save a nation, and he was convinced that if his fellow congressmen knew what happened that day they would surely support his cause.

His carefully prepared speech would follow one of the House's most brilliant orators, a thirty-three-year-old black congressman from South Carolina named Robert Elliott, a former soldier in the Union navy and a lawyer with a first-class education. Born in Boston to Jamaican parents, Elliott had spent much of his childhood on that Caribbean island. His academic career was financed by a wealthy Jamaican uncle, who sent him to London's High Holborn Academy, a prestigious private school. He graduated from Eton College in 1859, and received his law degree from Lincoln's Inn in London. After the war, he settled in Charleston, where he worked as a printer and associate editor of the *Missionary Record*. Before running for Congress, he practiced law, defending many former slaves.

As he stood before the House, Elliott said that, regrettably, his very dark complexion made it necessary to ask for his civil rights in Congress. He spoke in a measured melodic cadence, his sentences rising and falling in crescendo reminiscent of a minister's sermon. Elliott's powerful oratory—often accompanied by a sharp, acerbic, stinging wit—was now used with disarming civility to eviscerate Stephens and Harris, much to the delight of some members of the House and black onlookers in the gallery.

His sharpest words were reserved for Stephens.

"It is scarcely twelve years since that gentleman shocked the civilized world by announcing the birth of a government which rested on human slavery as its corner-stone," Elliott said of Stephens, who not only served as vice president in the Confederate government, but played a critical role in its creation. "The progress of events has swept away that pseudo-government which rested on greed, pride, and tyranny; and the race whom he then ruthlessly spurned and trampled on are here to meet him in debate, and to demand the rights which are enjoyed by their former oppressors, who vainly sought to overthrow a Government which they could not prostitute to the base uses of slavery."

Elliott's voice softened as he continued.

"The gentleman from Georgia has learned much since 1861; but he is still a laggard. Let him put away entirely the false and fatal theories which have so greatly marred an otherwise enviable record. Let him accept, in its fullness and beneficence, the great doctrine that American citizenship carries with it every civil and political right which manhood can confer. Let him lend his influence, with all his masterly ability, to complete the proud structure of legislation which makes his nation worthy of the great declaration which heralded its birth, and he will have done that which will most nearly redeem his reputation in the eyes of the world, and best vindicate the wisdom of that policy which has permitted him to regain his seat upon this floor."

Spurred on by cheers and laughter from the gallery, Elliott then turned his attention to Harris, who the day before had treated a black congressman with utter contempt. Elliott indicated that in a spirit of generosity he would refrain from striking Harris in his weakness, namely his ill-thought-out and indefensible position. Elliot said that although Harris made an invitingly easy target, he would grant the Virginia congressman the "mercy" of his silence.

Again the house exploded in applause, forcing the Speaker to vainly pound his gavel in an attempt to suppress it. Elliott then shifted to a scholarly tone. He launched into a lengthy legal analysis of the bill, arguing that Southern states had imposed such onerous burdens and inequities upon blacks that their freedom was of little value. A series of "black codes," or Jim Crow laws, had been enacted in the South to deny blacks the right to vote, serve on juries, testify against whites in court, or buy or lease real estate. Blacks were excluded from public schools, black orphans "apprenticed" to their former owners, and black servants required to work from dawn till dusk for their former masters.

Elliott argued that even a casual reading of the Thirteenth, Fourteenth, and Fifteenth Amendments clearly showed they were intended to secure the freedom of blacks. Making arguments that equal rights didn't mean equal protection was ludicrous, he contended. He also questioned why Southern blacks were denied their right to vote based on illiteracy. But the right to vote for illiterate white men in Kentucky had never been challenged, although according to 1870 U.S. Census figures, illiterate whites in Kentucky outnumbered nonreading blacks two to one.

The speech was followed by wild applause in the gallery, where black supporters shook hands in congratulations and cheered Elliott. House members from both sides of the aisle grabbed him by the shoulder and clasped his hand.

Congressman James B. Beck of Kentucky, a confirmed opponent of the bill, rose to defuse the effect of the speech with a backhanded compliment, saying it was wonderfully eloquent and certainly written by someone else. The next day, the *Chicago Ocean* newspaper wrote, "The honorable R. B. Elliott, the colored Congressman, has again persuaded that intellectual friend of his to write a speech for him. It would be well for more of our public men to engage the services of the same powerful writer."

By the time Butler rose to speak, he had listened to more than two and a half days of testimony. He found himself analyzing the legal merits of the case from both sides, a by-product of his career as a successful trial lawyer before the war. But he knew a legal response would not do today. He wasn't needed as lawyer or a politician. He needed to bear witness, to tell the world of the achievements he had seen on the battlefield by black soldiers.

There was a popular argument that blacks were the only race given their freedom by a decree, not by the shedding of their blood. Butler knew this to be untrue. Almost two hundred thousand black soldiers fought in the Civil War, and by the end of the ordeal, 10 percent of the Union army was black. The memory of dead soldiers on battlefields had not faded from his mind. He was aware that in the North there was a well of sympathy for the South in the postwar years. Many argued that the South needed to get back on its feet if the country was to prosper, and that the federal government should not meddle in its affairs. Many in the North were bored with Reconstruction. Even President Grant tired of it. The migration of blacks to the North caused racial tensions even in cities that never had slavery.

But all of these factors and complications didn't excuse the debt Butler felt had gone unpaid. Despite the sacrifice made by black soldiers and their families, they were still forced to come to Congress seeking their civil rights.

Butler knew these rights were hard-won. He had personally pinned Medals of Honor on the black troops who fought at New Market Heights. He still remembered their names: Christian Fleetwood, a shipping clerk from Baltimore; William H. Barnes, a farmer from St. Mary's County, Maryland; Powhatan Beaty, a farmer from Cincinnati; James H. Bronson, a barber from Delaware, Ohio; James Gardiner, an oyster fisherman from Gloucester, Virginia; James H. Harris, a farmer from St. Mary's County; Thomas R. Hawkins, a worker from Cincinnati; Alfred B. Hilton, a farmer from Harford County, Maryland; Milton M. Holland, a former slave from Austin, Texas; Miles James, a laborer from Princess Anne County, Virginia; Alexander Kelly, a coal miner from Saltsburg, Pennsylvania; Robert A. Pinn, a farmer from Stark County, Ohio; Edward Ratcliff, a laborer from James County, Virginia; and Charles Veal, a fireman from Portsmouth, Virginia.

As Butler acknowledged those in the gallery from his seat on the floor, he was mindful of the historical significance of the moment. The old general, whom colleagues once called the "Beast," was again preparing for battle. It was a different kind of battle, but Butler too was changed. The honorable representative from the state of Massachusetts no longer wore the bushy, untamed sideburns that had accentuated his wild dark eyes and seemed to characterize the rough manners that drew national attention during the conflict.

During those years of turmoil, General Butler's name had crossed nearly everyone's lips: in hushed prayers in the North, as a Moses among black Americans, and as a profanity or cuss word in the South. In the North he embodied the justness of the cause. In the South he personified Yankee vulgarity and the cruelties inflicted on the genteel Confederacy. His disdain for common civilities made him, in Southern eyes, less than chivalrous, and caused indignation from Richmond to as far away as London. His name spurred sympathy for the South even in foreign capitals where governments opposed slavery and generally frowned on civil wars. After he became captor of New Orleans, he insulted the entire South by issuing an order that any woman ridiculing or mocking a Union soldier should be considered a streetwalker plying her trade, and should be arrested on charges of solicitation. He hanged a man for removing a Union flag. That was when they began to refer to him as "the beast of New Orleans." The name stuck. Southern newspapers even carried characterizations of him with an animal's body and a tail.

Many still hadn't forgiven Butler a decade later, even if he looked less like a beast and more like a politician. A handlebar mustache now fell past the soft chin. His girth had expanded in the nine years since he left the rigors of military life for a comfortable seat in the House. But the coarse administrative style, which admirers dismissed as righteous zeal, hadn't mellowed. He was still as likely to insult as astonish. Whatever the reason, the former Democrat turned general turned radical Republican still caused gasps and whispers among some of his colleagues on the floor.

As Butler stood before the House, striking a pose eerily similar to a general reviewing his troops, he was clearly ready to battle all comers.

He opened by saying the bill was not an attempt to make everyone and everything equal. Butler said he didn't believe that all men were created equal, if the word was to be used in the broad sense. Some were born healthy and strong, talented and intelligent. Others were not.

But every man had the right to be the equal of every other man, if God had given him that power. The bill only removed the man-made impediments. For instance, he said, God had clearly given Congressman Elliott the power to be equal in eloquence to the proudest man on the floor of the House. Yet, as the debate over the issue also demonstrated, God didn't give everyone on the floor the power to be the equal of Elliott. This remark brought a loud applause from the floor and the gallery.

Butler smirked at the argument that a civil rights bill would destroy the Southern school system. The South had no common school system before the war, he said, and what did exist was considered feeble at best. He quoted antebellum educational authorities who said the only schools in the South were for paupers or the affluent, and those were not common schools.

He ridiculed the objections that been made to the bill on the grounds that whites in the South would object to riding the same railroad cars with blacks. Unless tradition was a liar, he said, many whites and blacks of the South shared the same fathers. But his tone turned reverent and serious as he shifted the focus to the Civil War and the heroism he witnessed at New Market Heights.

No battle during the U.S. Civil War saw such a stunning display of heroics and gallantry from black soldiers as that fought the morning of September 29, 1864, on the rolling hills of rural Virginia. Of the sixteen black Congressional Medal of Honor winners during the war, fourteen received the citation for gallantry displayed that day. At the break of dawn, the columns of black soldiers walked directly into the line of enemy fire under a hail of bullets. Butler could remember the scene clearly in his mind and described it in detail to the House.

"There, in a space not wider than the clerk's desk, and three hundred yards long, lay the dead bodies of 543 of my colored comrades, slain in the defense of their country, who had laid down their lives to uphold its flag and its honor, as a willing sacrifice. And as I rode along, guiding my horse this way and that, lest he should profane with his hoofs what seemed to me the sacred dead, and as I looked at their bronzed faces upturned in the shining sun, as if in mute appeal against the wrongs of the country for which they had given their lives, and whose flag had been to them a flag of stripes, in which no star of glory had ever shone for them—feeling I had wronged them in the past, and believing what was the future duty of my country to them—I swore to myself a solemn oath: 'May my right hand forget its cunning, and my tongue cleave to the roof of my mouth, if ever I fail to defend the rights of the men who have given their blood for me and my country this day and for their race forever.' And, God helping me, I will keep that oath."

Butler's words had a strange impact on the House. There was a sudden hush, as if congressmen and audience alike had decided at that precise moment to collectively hold their breath or engage in some deep and profound thought that required complete and utter silence.

That day on the battlefield, Butler went on to say, changed him forever. His prejudices against the black race up to that time all departed that moment, seeing the fallen black soldiers. "The Old-time States-rights Democrat disappeared," he said.

Butler admitted he became a thorough Negro lover, and avowed before the world that as long as their rights were not equal to those of other men on the continent, he was "on their side against all comers."

The former general pleaded with opponents of the bill to get over their prejudices as he had gotten over his. "These men had fought for their country. They had shown themselves in battle the equal to whites, they had shown themselves as citizens to be docile, quiet, kind, temperate and laborious. They had knowledge, bravery, culture, power and eloquence, and who should say that they should not have what the Constitution gave them? Equal rights."

Another round of loud and continuous applause erupted from the galleries and the floor, broken in measure by the loud percussive hammering of the gavel by the Speaker.

Butler's speech made the heroics displayed at New Market Heights officially part of the congressional record. It would serve as irrefutable proof of the bravery not only of those wounded or silenced on the battlefield, but of an entire race.

The bill for which Butler, Elliott, and others fought became law the following year. But the victory for blacks and their supporters was short-lived. Eight years later, the U.S. Supreme Court ruled the law unconstitutional and the South quickly began enforcing the old Jim Crow laws with renewed vigor.

History too would prove unkind. The battles of Atlanta, Bull Run, and Gettysburg would be far better remembered and more talked about. But for those who fought at New Market Heights or lost loved ones in the fields near the old farmhouses, no battlefield was more hallowed, no dead more sacred.

ONE

THE BELL TOLLS
A Call for Black Troops

O n July 6, 1863, three days after the terrible fighting at Gettysburg, Christian Fleetwood saw the gaunt, soiled faces of the defeated, walking as shattered men through his hometown of Baltimore. About nineteen thousand rebel prisoners were marched through the city's narrow cobblestone streets that day, the pain and horror of the war reflected in their drawn faces and unseeing eyes.

Horse-drawn ambulances carrying the wounded, some crying in pain, descended upon the town along with hundreds of grim-faced Union soldiers, many still in a state of shock. The ugly aftermath of the battle was evident everywhere as a dark gloom wrapped the city.

For Fleetwood and others in Baltimore, the war that once seemed so distant was suddenly too close to ignore. For months, Fleetwood weighed the decision of whether to join the fight; now that decision would be tempered by the stark reality of the scene unfolding before his eyes. Gone were any romantic notions of the war. The faces of the vanquished and victors held no sign of glory, only the vestiges of a brutal struggle that left them somehow less human.

Gettysburg, like some grim reaper, had exacted its toll. The numbers were staggering. The Union army lost twenty-three thousand soldiers killed, wounded, or missing in the three days of fighting, the South another twenty thousand. News from the battlefront dominated the newspapers. War correspondents from all over the country were in Baltimore that day, relaying dispatches back to editors. They told their stories in bars and taverns. People strained to listen.

The reporters told of a mad, daring charge across an open plain by the Confederate army on the third and final day of the battle. They told of how Union soldiers waited until the enemy drew near, then unleashed deadly cannon and musket fire. Hundreds of the helpless rebels fell as the air filled with smoke, the acrid smell of gunpowder, and cries of death. But the fractured rebel lines kept charging, finally reaching the outer fringe of the Union army.

One eyewitness recounted the battle: "Men fire into each other's faces, not five feet apart. There are bayonet-thrusts, saber-strokes, pistol-shots . . . men going down on their hands and knees, spinning round like tops, throwing out their arms, gulping up blood, falling; legless, armless, headless. There are ghastly heaps of men."

The brutality of the slaughter, which ended with the retreat of Southern troops, was never equaled in the war. The North claimed victory, but there was hardly celebration.

As a clerk, Fleetwood knew what the loss of so many soldiers would ultimately mean. The ledgers would demand that the North put out a call for more troops to replace those who lay dead or wounded in Pennsylvania. The very complexion of the war was changing. It was no longer a white man's fight about states' rights. The death rolls reached into every town and village, and now an invitation to join the carnage was being extended to black recruits. After two years of spurning black soldiers, the Union, Fleetwood knew, could no longer afford to turn them away.

Throughout that July day, the sobering news of Gettysburg was on everyone's lips in the city of 212,000. Residents stood stoically in line for broadsheets listing the dead. Shrieks of anguish reverberated through the shuttered streets as the names of loved ones were recognized, augmenting the pervasive air of sadness and melancholy that settled on the city. With no decisive victory for Union forces, the battle that so many in the North hoped would end the war merely made it more unbearable.

With Lee's army escaping south to the Potomac River en route to Virginia, it was clear the war was far from over. Now the gluttonous, unending conflict would demand more troops to replace the fallen.

Federal recruiters seeking to enlist blacks arrived in Fleetwood's hometown on July 6, the very day the wounded began arriving from Gettysburg. Strange as it would have seemed just a year earlier, the recruiters offered freedom to slaves, honor to free persons of color, and the possibility of limited advancement in the ranks of the Union army for all blacks.

But Fleetwood wasn't a slave; he never worked on a plantation or as a servant. He wasn't convinced that this was his fight. Besides, at five feet four inches and 125 pounds, the well-read, articulate, and cultured Fleetwood was an unlikely candidate for the rigors of military life. He had plans to travel to Liberia in the fall to join a colony of blacks who wanted to live free of racial prejudice. These plans had been given a new sense of urgency by President Lincoln's decision earlier in the year to normalize diplomatic relations with Liberia and encourage blacks to migrate to the African country.

At twenty-three, Fleetwood had a comfortable job as a clerk in a Baltimore shipyard. His circle of friends included influential, progressive-thinking blacks in Baltimore, the city where former slave and abolitionist Frederick Douglass had grown up a generation earlier. Fleetwood was a founding member of the first black journal in the Maryland region, the *Lyceum Observer*, a forum for black interests, including the advancement of black rights. He was also a regular contributor to the *Christian Recorder*, a newspaper published by the Episcopal Church.

Fleetwood and his friends had rigorous, heated debates—often into the wee hours of the morning—about religion, politics, physics, literature, civil rights, and the war. He felt at ease in intellectual circles. A musician, choirmaster, and singer in the church, he often dotted his letters with the French expressions and Latin phrases of the well educated. Soft-spoken and friendly, with curious eyes that lit up when he smiled, Fleetwood possessed a combination of affable traits that appealed to a wide circle of friends as well as his superiors and leaders in Baltimore. Clergy of the Episcopal Church in town considered him a leading candidate for a rectory.

But always, Fleetwood was reminded that the seeming normalcy of his life was an illusion. He was black, and that fact alone relegated him to a prison without walls that offered a confinement as sure as any four-by-four cell.

Fleetwood's driving ambition made it difficult for him to accept the stifling limitations of life for blacks in America. He had traveled abroad and was painfully aware that another world existed outside America where things were different. With each new racial insult, his sense of disillusionment with his homeland was heightened, as was his interest in moving to Africa.

His education began at the home of a wealthy sugar merchant, John C. Burns, and his wife, who were particularly fond of the engaging young man. It continued at the office of the secretary of the Maryland Colonization Society, an organization dedicated to ending slavery by repatriating blacks to Africa. At sixteen, Fleetwood had traveled to Liberia and Sierra Leone. In 1860, he graduated from the all-black Ashman Institute, later renamed Lincoln University, in Pennsylvania. As a black, he was automatically denied admission to most colleges in the state. Once again, Fleetwood experienced the keen impress of prejudice, standing by while far less talented whites entered universities whose doors remained firmly shut in his face.

He understood injustice in the intimate, personal way of the discriminated against. And while he struggled with his role in the war, there was no debate in his heart about the need to break through the barriers that not only prevented blacks from advancing, but kept many in physical bondage. This was especially true in his hometown of Baltimore.

Baltimore was a slave-owning town rife with prejudice. Sympathies lay as much with the South as the North. On April 19, 1861, in the opening days of the war, a large group of pro-Southern townsmen—some carrying Confederate flags—provoked an exchange of gunfire with the 6th Massachusetts Volunteers as they passed through the city on their way to Washington, D.C.

The ugly mob, throwing bricks, bottles, stones, and just about anything they could get their hands on, stormed the railway cars carrying the troops. Nine cars escaped, but the tenth was pushed off the tracks. With the situation becoming more explosive by the moment, the soldiers in the derailed car tried marching to the next station. The seething mob followed, pressing closer. Suddenly, several people in the crowd opened fire, and within minutes four Union soldiers lay dead in the streets of Baltimore, another thirty-nine wounded. That evening, Fleetwood could see the billowing smoke and amber glow of fires around the city as residents burned bridges to prevent more soldiers from going through their town to Washington. A day later, President Lincoln suspended all troop movements through Baltimore. The 6th Massachusetts returned a few days later and occupied Federal Hill overlooking the city.

Now, two years after the riot, little had changed in Fleetwood's hometown, where residents were still as likely to cheer for the Confederate army as for the Union. Faced with this reality, Union troops treated Baltimore as an occupied city for the duration of the war.

With Baltimore now the site of active recruitment of blacks, one of the foremost questions on Fleetwood's mind was the role blacks would play in the Union army. One thing was clear: they would fight under white commanders. But would they be considered expendable and thrown into the heaviest fire?

Fleetwood, like other blacks, had been unable to enlist for much of the war. He had watched from the sidelines, wondering how the conflict would affect life for black Americans. Many blacks viewed the struggle with intellectual indifference, believing it had little to do with them. Indeed, until the conflict began to take a heavy toll in lives, the abolition of slavery was an underlying but not primary issue.

Nine months before Gettysburg, President Lincoln stated unequivocally that the war was not about the slavery issue. "My paramount aim in this struggle is to save the Union, and is not either to save or destroy slavery," the president wrote in an open letter to Horace Greeley, editor of the *New York Tribune*. "If I could either save the Union without freeing any slaves, I would do it, and if I could save it by freeing all the slaves I would do it; and if I could save it by freeing some and leaving others alone I would also do that."

Fleetwood was among those who cheered when Lincoln's Emancipation Proclamation freed the slaves in the rebel states in January 1863. But his heart sank when that freedom wasn't extended to the states under Lincoln's and the Union's control. Maryland remained a slave state—Lincoln didn't dare offend pro-Union slave states by setting blacks free in their territories. Fleetwood, seeing the shackles of his brethren in his own town, questioned why should he fight to preserve a union that would not guarantee the freedom of all blacks. Finding no suitable answer, the military seemed an illogical vocation. With a heavy heart, his thoughts remained fixed on Liberia.

To attract blacks the military began placing recruitment posters in Baltimore and other cities. The large, bold print was disturbingly reminiscent of notices for slave auctions: "Men of Color, To Arms! To Arms! Now or Never. Three Year's Service. Battles of Liberty and the Union. Fail Now & Our Race is Doomed."

With a number of slaves enlisting in hopes of obtaining their freedom, some posters addressed free blacks with a nagging question: "Are Freemen less Brave than Slaves?"

Fleetwood felt that doubts and disparaging comments about the courage of blacks were unfair. Blacks had shown a willingness to fight, but were rebuffed by the stubbornness of the Union to accept black soldiers. Fleetwood would later tell friends, "The North came slowly and reluctantly to recognize the Negro as a factor for good in the war. 'This is a white man's war' met the Negroes at every step of their first efforts to gain admission to the armies of the Union."

The willingness of blacks to fight was evidenced early in the war. But it was the South, not the North, that first enlisted them, a fact that deeply disturbed Fleetwood. Although the Confederacy enlisted blacks for support detail, not as armed combatants, the irony was not wasted on him.

Two weeks after the fall of Fort Sumter in April 1861, at the very start of the war, the *Charleston Mercury* had reported the passing through Augusta, Georgia, of several companies of rebel troops, including the 3rd and 4th Georgia regiments, fifteen other white companies, and one Negro company from Nashville, Tennessee. And a telegram from New Orleans dated November 23, 1861, noted the review by Governor Thomas Moore of more than 28,000 troops, including one regiment comprised of "1,400 colored men." Some Southern newspapers even praised the black soldiers. The *New Orleans Picayune*, referring to a military review held February 9, 1862, stated, "We must also pay a deserved compliment to the companies of free colored men, all very well drilled and comfortably equipped."

Yet it did not escape Fleetwood that during the evacuation of New Orleans two months later, all of the Southern troops succeeded in getting away except the black troops. "They got left," he noted sarcastically.

The attitude toward enlisting blacks was rapidly changing in the North. Just days after Gettysburg, at a recruiting station in Baltimore, Union major general Robert Schenck received a dispatch from Washington ordering him to start recruiting blacks. The notice, from Secretary of War Edward M. Stanton, read, "The chief of Bureau for Organizing Colored Troops will issue an order for organizing a regiment in your department, and Colonel Birney has been directed to report to you immediately for that duty. The chief of the Bureau will furnish instructions."

The Union's decision to enlist blacks raised a critical question: should runaway slaves from the South be allowed to join Union forces?

In the early months of the war, the Union leaders wanted to turn away escaped slaves. General Benjamin Butler, fighting near Fort Monroe in Virginia, disagreed. He believed the Union should deprive the South of any manpower at its disposal, including slaves. The Confederate commander opposing Butler's troops was using slaves to help build fortifications. Butler wrote President Lincoln that escaped slaves should be treated the same as any other property taken from the Confederate army.

"Twelve of these Negroes have escaped from the erection of batteries on Sewall's point, which this morning fired upon my expedition as it passed by out of range. As a means of offense therefore in the enemy's hands these Negroes are of importance. Without them, the batteries could not have been erected at least for many weeks. It would seem to be a measure of necessity to deprive their masters of their services."

Butler declared escaped slaves as "contrabands of war," or riches over which slave owners lost claim when they rebelled. Lincoln approved of this policy, maintaining that it was not a policy toward abolition but a tactic of war to save lives of Northern soldiers.

Frederick Douglass, a former slave himself, objected to the term as bitterly distasteful. "Contraband sounds more like a pistol than a human being." But the policy changed the underlying meaning of the war. Suddenly the fight was helping thousands of blacks gain freedom. Escaped slaves began showing up at Union camps referring to themselves as "contraband."

Butler's decision aside, no man in Fleetwood's eyes was more responsible for changing public opinion in the North about black troops than Union general David Hunter. Hunter's effort to form a black regiment in South Carolina in the spring of 1862 was well-known.

Hunter's arming of blacks, many of them runaway slaves, sent political shock waves through the North, especially in Congress, where critics of the general's policy existed on both sides of the aisle. The Lincoln administration, Fleetwood noted, stayed out of the fray and let the general handle his critics. He proved quite capable.

Congressman Charles A. Wickliffe of Kentucky issued a resolution before the House asking that Hunter answer for his actions. "Resolved, That the Secretary of War be directed to inform this House if General Hunter, of the department of South Carolina, has organized a regiment of South Carolina volunteers for the defense of the Union, composed of black men [fugitive slaves], and appointed the colonel and other officers to command them." Wickliffe argued that Hunter had no authority to enlist black soldiers or give them arms, clothing, and equipment. House members approved the resolution on June 9, 1862.

Secretary of War Stanton disavowed any involvement or knowledge of Hunter's actions. That might have put the matter to rest. But General Hunter was not easily cornered. He wrote back to Stanton, who eagerly passed the reply on to the House, where Hunter's critics lay in wait. Congressman Samuel Cox was looking for a campaign issue for the upcoming election. A speech, he believed, railing against the threat of armed black troops would provide him with "first-rate Democratic thunder." As the clerk of the House rose to announce the letter, Cox caught the Speaker's eye and signaled that he wanted to be booked for the first speech against what was being called "The Negro Experiment."

Hunter's letter began politely enough by repeating the questions addressed to him. Had he organized a regiment of fugitive slaves? Did he have the authority to do so? Had he furnished them with arms, clothing, and equipment?

Cox rubbed his hands in anticipation, nodding knowingly to a supporter. The clerk continued reading.

"Only having received the letter conveying the inquiries at a late hour on Saturday night, I urge forward my answer in time for the steamer sailing today [Monday], this haste preventing me from entering as minutely as I could wish upon many points of detail, such as the paramount importance of the subject calls for."

Cox listened intently, leaning forward to catch each word. The clerk went on: "But in view of the near termination of the present session of Congress, and the widespread interest which must have been awakened by Mr. Wickliffe's resolution, I prefer sending even this imperfect answer to waiting the period necessary for the collection of fuller and more comprehensive data."

A brief smile played across Cox's face, expiring before reaching his eyes. If Hunter planned to try to weasel out of an indefensible position, Cox had no intention of letting him. But the crafty general had no such plans, as Cox was about to discover.

Hunter explained that he hadn't raised any regiment of "fugitive slaves." More precisely, "There is, however, a fine regiment of persons whose late masters are 'fugitive rebels,' men who everywhere fly before the appearance of the national flag, leaving their servants behind them to shift as best they can for themselves. So far, indeed, are the loyal persons composing this regiment from seeking to avoid the presence of their late owners that they are now, one and all, working with remarkable industry to place themselves in a position to go in full and effective pursuit of their fugacious and traitorous proprietors."

Cox shifted uncomfortably in his seat. Things weren't going according to plan. Over applause and laughter, the clerk carried on, his voice growing louder over the din.

Hunter believed he was authorized to enlist "fugitive slaves" as soldiers. But he couldn't find anyone of that description. "No such characters have, however, yet appeared within our most advanced pickets, the loyal slaves everywhere remaining on their plantations to welcome us, and supply us with food, labor and information. It is the masters who have, in every instance, been the 'fugitives'—running away from loyal slaves as well as loyal soldiers, and whom we have only partially been able to see—chiefly their heads over ramparts, or, rifle in hand, dodging behind trees, in the extreme distance."

By now, the mood on the floor was one of levity and outright hilarity, with the exception of Representative Wickliffe. Even Cox found himself unable to hold back a smile.

Hunter's words continued:

"In the absence of any 'fugitive master' law, the deserted slaves would be wholly without remedy, had not the crime of treason given them the right to pursue, capture, and bring back those persons of whose protection they have been thus suddenly bereft."

As to the question of whether Hunter issued clothes, uniforms, arms, equipment, etc., such authority is implied, he said. "Neither have I had any specific authority for supplying these persons with shovels, spades and pickaxes when employing them as laborers, nor with boats and oars when using them as lighter men; but these are not points included in [the House's] resolution. To me it seemed that liberty to employ men in any particular capacity implied with it liberty also to supply them with the necessary tools; and acting under this faith I have clothed, equipped and armed the only loyal regiment yet raised in South Carolina."

Hunter apologized profusely to the House that demands on his time allowed him to raise only one such regiment instead of five. "The experiment of arming the blacks, so far as I have made it, has been a complete and even marvelous success. They are sober, docile, attentive, and enthusiastic, displaying great natural capacities for acquiring the duties of a soldier. They are eager beyond all things to take the field and be led into action; and it is the unanimous opinion of the officers who have had charge of them, that in the peculiarities of this climate and country, they will prove invaluable auxiliaries, fully equal to the similar regiments so long and successfully used by the British authorities in the West Indies."

Cox and Wickliffe had been outflanked. "I tell you that letter from Hunter spoiled the prettiest speech I had ever thought of making," Cox said afterward. "Well you see, man proposes, but Providence orders otherwise."

Cox canceled his speech. "Before the document was concluded, I motioned to the Speaker that he might give the floor to whom he pleased, as my desire to distinguish myself in that particular tilt was over."

Hunter's brilliant argument, dripping with sarcasm, allowed him to avoid a carefully laid trap by savvy political enemies and press forward with the enlistment of blacks. In his cause, the general found an unlikely ally in a rough-spoken white soldier by the name of Colonel "Miles O'Reilly" Halpine, of the old 10th Army Corps. Fleetwood credited a popular ditty written by Halpine with helping end reservations in the North over the use of black soldiers. The coarse ditty, reflecting the vulgar prejudices of the time, summed up the sentiments of many whites:

> Some say it is a burning shame to make the Naygurs fight,
> An' that the trade o' being kilt belongs but to the white:
> But as for me, upon me sowl, so liberal are we here,
> I'll let Sambo be murthered, in place of meself, on every day
>   of the year.

On every day of the year, boys, and every hour in the day,
The right to be kilt I'll divide wid him, and divil a word I'll
	say.
In battles wild commotion I shouldn't at all object,
If Sambo's body should stop a ball that was coming for me
	direct,
An' the prod of a southern bayonet, so liberal are we here,
I'll resign and let Sambo take it, on every day in the year.
On every day in the year, boys, an' wid none of your nasty
	pride,
All right in a southern bagnet prod, wid Sambo I'll divide.
The men who object to Sambo, should take his place and
	fight,
An' it is better to have a Naygur's hue, than a liver that's
	weak an' white.
Though Sambo's black as the ace of spades, his finger a
	thryger can pull,
An' his eye runs straight on the barrel sight from under its
	thatch of wool.
So hear me all, boys, darlin, don't think I'm tipping you
	chaff,
The right to be kilt, I'll divide with him, an' give him the
	largest half.

By the summer of 1863, black soldiers were marching in the
streets of several cities, something that would have been
unheard of just a short time before. And a War Department
order offering freedom to all slaves who enlisted opened a flood-
gate of blacks willing to take up arms and fight for the Union.

Fleetwood had no illusions. The black enlistments were
driven by political necessity, not a newfound sense of racial sen-
sitivity or political conscience.

Frederick Douglass used his influence as a famous black orator on a recruiting tour of Northern cities in March to get blacks to enlist in the U.S. Army. Both of his sons, Charles and Lewis, enlisted in the 54th U.S. Colored Infantry.

"Who would be free themselves must strike the blow," Douglass told his fellow blacks. "I urge you to fly to arms and smite to death the power that would bury the Government and your liberty in the same hopeless grave. This is your golden opportunity."

Douglass instinctively felt that military service would change the status of blacks. He had argued since the beginning of the war for the use of black regiments. "Once you let the black man get upon his person the brass letter, U.S., let him get an eagle on his button, and a musket on his shoulder and bullets in his pocket, there is no power on earth that can deny that he has earned the right to citizenship." He disagreed with President Lincoln that blacks should return to Africa and colonize Liberia. "The colored race can never be respected until they are respected in America."

Douglass's arguments for enlistment gave Fleetwood a new perspective on the war. If Douglass was right, blacks could earn rights on the battlefield that had been denied them by legislatures across the country.

But while Douglass articulated intellectual reasons for blacks to join the war, the conflict was losing support among whites, who were fleeing the horrors of the battlefield and deserting at the rate of 152 a day. There was even open opposition to a federal draft.

What began as a slow, smoldering anger against the draft exploded into violence one week after Gettysburg when the names of the first federal draftees were drawn in New York and published in newspapers across the country. The draft struck a raw nerve in America's grandest city, especially over the provision that allowed a draftee to buy an exemption or have someone else do his military duty. It was "a rich man's war and a poor man's fight," protesters cried. Politicians who didn't support the war stoked the discontent by railing against the draft.

On July 13, two days after the first names were drawn, many of those drafted arrived in New York with their families and friends. They gathered in vacant lots, carrying weapons, clubs, cart rungs, pieces of iron. The swelling crowd moved to Central Park and then headed for the draft offices. As the drawing of names continued, the mob closed in. Within minutes of their gathering, a full-scale riot developed. The draft headquarters was stormed and residences raided. Vandals looted businesses. The angry crowd overpowered police, firemen, and soldiers. The carnage spread throughout the city. A black church and orphanage were burned. The unrest continued for three days.

A *New York Times* report on the third day captured the chaos: "The ravages of the mob which commenced its diabolical career on Monday are not ended, and it is impossible to say at the hour of going to press this morning whether the worst has yet been seen. All through Tuesday night marauding bands of plunderers continued to commit their depredations in various parts of the city, but at daylight yesterday morning they had generally dispersed and there was a fair prospect of a speedy restoration of quiet and order. The authorities both state and military, appeared to consider the riot as substantially subdued."

Blacks, the city's most defenseless residents, bore the brunt of the attacks. The *Times* reported, "At a late hour on Tuesday night the mob made an attack upon the tenement houses, occupied by colored people, in Sullivan and Thompson streets. For three hours, and up to two o'clock yesterday morning there was what may be truly said to be a 'reign of terror' throughout all that portion of the city. Several buildings were fired, and a large number of colored persons were beaten so badly that they lay insensible in the street for hours after. Two colored children at No. 59 Thompson Street were shot and instantly killed."

Secretary of War Stanton sent a dispatch to New York City mayor George Updike pledging help. "Five regiments are under orders to return to New York. The retreat of Lee [at Gettysburg], having now become a rout, with his army broken and much heavier loss of killed and wounded than was supposed, will relieve a larger force for the restoration of order in New York."

As disheartening as Fleetwood found the attacks on blacks during the New York riots, he was about to get another dose of bad news. This time it would involve a significant loss of life among one of the North's most vaunted black regiments.

A week after the New York riots, Union soldiers, headed by the 54th Massachusetts Colored Infantry, made an unsuccessful attack on Fort Wagner in South Carolina. The black regiment was assigned to lead the attack. As the Union troops formed on the beach, ready for the assault, the order to advance was withheld until the 54th could march by and take position at the head of the column. The regiment charged the embankment around the fort, unshielded from rebel fire. Hundreds of soldiers were killed. But Colonel Shaw, the white commander of the regiment, and several of his men were able to breach the parapet before falling dead. Of 650 soldiers in the regiment, 279 were lost.

The news sent shock waves through black communities across the country. Many, Fleetwood included, felt the regiment had been honored to lead the battle. Their sacrifice to their country and the Union cause was beyond question. But the battle also touched an underlying fear that black troops would be placed in the most dangerous situations where commanders wouldn't order white troops to go.

On July 21, three days after the battle, President Lincoln ordered recruiters to step up the enlistment of black soldiers. And even in the wake of the tragedy at Fort Wagner, blacks continued to answer the call and line up for service.

As Fleetwood contemplated recent events, fate was about to intervene in his life. The war disrupted trade with Liberia, ending his hope of traveling there in the near future. His options suddenly curtailed, he reconsidered the military. He mulled over the arguments of Douglass and others on why blacks should enlist, spending many evenings in deep soul-searching. Invariably, his thoughts returned to the shuffling, broken men he witnessed returning from Gettysburg. He had seen the casualties of war, knew that glory was sometimes won with limb or life, yet he was now more certain than ever of what he had to do. Some things, he concluded, were worth dying for.

On a humid morning in August 1863, with the sweltering breath of summer cascading beads of sweat down his face and open shirt, Christian Fleetwood walked into an army recruiting center in Baltimore. Drawn by high ideals, he had come to fight, and possibly die, for the Union and his race. He had no way to foretell the future. But long before the bloody conflict ended, the shipping clerk from Baltimore would find his courage and mettle tested beyond his most terrifying imaginings.

TWO

CHRISTIAN FLEETWOOD ENLISTS

The day Fleetwood walked into the enlistment station at Camp Birney, the outcome of the war was as uncertain as the day it began. One hundred miles to the south in the Confederate capital of Richmond, Jefferson Davis that day refused the resignation of a grief-stricken General Robert E. Lee, who accepted the blame for the defeat at Gettysburg. "Our country could not bear to lose you," Davis wrote Lee.

President Lincoln was still defending his draft policy to Governor Horatio Seymour of New York just weeks after the draft riots. Antiwar Democrats cried for peace and tried pressuring Congress to negotiate an end to the bloody conflict with the South. A small but vocal minority supported such an agreement even if it meant accepting the independence of the Confederacy and the end of the Union.

But amid cries for peace and appeasement, the war continued. At Fort Sumter, where the war opened two years earlier, Confederate guns bombarded Union positions on Morris Island.

The attack was joined by the battery at Fort Wagner where, just weeks earlier, the black troops of the 54th Massachusetts fought and fell in a furious, glorious charge.

In Fleetwood's hometown, blacks were now actively recruited for military service. Major General Robert C. Schenck and Colonel William Birney were in Baltimore organizing the 4th U.S. Colored Troops. Their orders came from the secretary of war and the president himself.

Fleetwood, having reconciled himself to the anticipated rigors of military life, joined dozens of fresh-faced black recruits eager to serve. They arrived from all walks of life: farmers, laborers, clergy, ex-slaves, each with his own unique story and motive for enlisting. Fleetwood's name added clerk, newspaperman, choirmaster, and idealist to the list.

The war was a great foraging beast that would consume many of the new recruits, altering their lives as irreversibly as it was changing the political landscape of America. More than forty thousand blacks would die in uniform, most of disease, but nearly three thousand would be killed by enemy fire. The survivors, too, would not escape unscathed, many leaving the battlefield physically broken and psychologically scarred. In August 1863, the war's insatiable appetite for death and carnage was in full evidence from as far west as Texas and Missouri to the eastern seaboard, where rebel seamen constantly sought to evade the Union's blockade of international sea trade with the South.

Fleetwood enlisted on August 11, the same day as Alfred B. Hilton, a twenty-one-year-old, heavily muscled farmer from Harford County, Maryland. Hilton was living near Camp Birney on his father's farm on Gavel Hill Road when he decided to join the Union army. He was immediately given the rank of sergeant. Years of farming and hard work helped sculpt Hilton into an impressive physical figure. Fleetwood found him "a magnificent specimen of a man, over six feet tall and splendidly proportioned."

Also in the unit was Charles Veal, who, like Fleetwood and Hilton, would see action at New Market Heights. Veal, who enlisted two weeks before Fleetwood and Hilton, was a diminutive twenty-five-year-old Baltimore fireman born in Portsmouth, Virginia. He stood just five feet three inches tall. Fleetwood, always conscious about his own height, felt a kinship with the little fireman. "We were both such little fellows," he noted. "I think I weighed then about 125 pounds, and he about the same."

Fleetwood, Hilton, Veal, and the other recruits underwent a cursory medical exam and were put through a series of simple physical tests to determine their fitness for duty. The medical examinations for Union and Confederate enlistees were so notoriously superficial that a number of women enlisted as men and avoided discovery until wounded or captured. Some were never exposed until years after their discharge.

The physical tests included a demonstration that the enlistee could bite open a cartridge for his rifle. The recruiting board, comprised of officers, was often infinitely easy to please. With the war's hunger for new recruits, few enlistees were turned away. Once accepted, the men were issued a uniform, along with a knapsack, haversack, canteen, blanket, knife, fork, spoon, tin cup, and tin plate.

At a time when many recruits—both blacks and whites—were barely literate, Fleetwood's and Hilton's education and skills impressed the recruiters. Normally, men of their background could hope for a commission. But blacks could not be appointed commissioned officers. Army guidelines, however, allowed the best and brightest among the black troops to be given the rank of noncommissioned officers within their units. Fleetwood and Hilton easily qualified for such positions.

Fleetwood was given the rank of sergeant. Eight days later, he was promoted to sergeant major. This meteoric rise presented something of a bitter irony for him. Although he welcomed the advancement, just a week into the army he had achieved the highest rank a black soldier could obtain. Had he been white, he almost certainly would have been able to obtain a commission. Overqualified and undervalued at the same time, he was assigned some of the clerical duties for the regiment.

The illogic of his predicament wasn't wasted on Fleetwood. He enlisted to strike a blow to slavery, a cornerstone of which was the commonly held belief in the inferiority of blacks. But even as a Union soldier, that very ingrained prejudice prevented him from assuming a position of command for which he was eminently suited.

Fleetwood's fellow enlistees were an eclectic assortment of characters. Some were free blacks from the area, others escaped slaves. They had willingly signed up although the perils of military life were well documented. Newspapers abounded with stories of deprivation and infectious diseases among troops, both of which proved more deadly than enemy fire. By the end of the conflict, 110,100 Union soldiers—black and white—would fall in the heat of battle or of wounds, and 224,580 more would succumb to diseases such as typhoid, dysentery, and measles.

Nevertheless, for the runaway slave, these dangers paled in comparison to the promise of liberty offered by military service. But even in uniform, the escaped slave had no surety of freedom. Runaway-slave enlistees were constantly reminded that their right to freedom could be easily challenged by their old masters. Slave owners would gather at the camp to pore over enlistment rolls in search of escaped slaves. An army board was set up to investigate the claims and examine documentation provided by slave owners. If an owner consented to allow his slave to enlist, the slave was freed forever and the owner was paid three hundred dollars in compensation. If a slave owner wouldn't consent to part with his property, the slave was returned to him.

Lincoln himself weighed in on the policy. In response to a letter from Secretary of War Stanton asking for clarification on the enlisting of slaves, his response was unequivocal. "To the recruiting of slaves of disloyal owners, no objection," the president wrote. "To recruiting slaves of loyal owners with their consent, no objection."

But Lincoln said he did object to "recruiting slaves of loyal owners, without consent . . . unless necessity is urgent." The president also opposed aggressive recruiting techniques, including the enlistment of slaves who normally didn't meet military requirements. It was clear that Lincoln was taking into consideration the sensitivities of the increasingly alarmed pro-Union slave owners.

New recruits claimed by slave owners and hauled away to renewed bondage had no recourse. No one with the power to help came to their defense. Not the courts, which had consistently upheld slave owners' rights; not the president, eager to appease slave owners loyal to the Union. Compounding the injustice was the knowledge that those reclaimed to slavery were being denied the opportunity to strike a blow against the hated institution that held them hostage.

For the runaway slave it was the final ignominy. Even after enlisting to serve his country, his freedom remained as tenuous as that of an escaped convict who must repeatedly look behind or cringe in fear when his name is shouted from the dark.

For Fleetwood and other free blacks, the slave master's claim held no personal threat. But few could stomach seeing their black fellow enlistees hauled off in so cruel a fashion to so cruel a fate. And while their protests often amounted to little more than muted, under-the-breath mutterings, no black soldier, Fleetwood included, had any illusions that admission into the army meant equality.

It was a particular affront to Fleetwood, whose primary reason for enlisting was the grand goal of helping destroy slavery and ending discrimination. He enlisted willing to die for a cause he saw as glorious, but the disconcerting treatment of runaway slaves—coupled with the limited opportunity for advancement for black soldiers—tarnished that cause and left lingering doubts as to the true intentions of the federal government for which he fought.

Slave owners saw things very differently. Some complained bitterly about the zeal of the man in charge of recruiting black soldiers.

Colonel William Birney was an aggressive recruiter who planned to raise seven regiments, each with almost a thousand black soldiers. A trained attorney, he saw enlistment as a way to free slaves and further the abolitionist cause—his goal was to free as many as possible. He was the forty-four-year-old son of abolitionist leader James G. Birney and shared his father's passion and conviction against slavery. Birney was born in the heart of the South in Huntsville, Alabama, and was educated at Centre College and Yale. He later spent five years in Europe. In France, he joined the revolution of 1848 and afterward was appointed professor of English at the University of Paris. At the outbreak of the Civil War, the warrior scholar was commissioned captain. His brother James was also a rising commander in the Union army.

William Birney had distinguished himself on several battlefields. He fought in both Bull Run battles and was promoted to major. He also fought at Chantilly and Fredericksburg. In January, he had been promoted to colonel.

In gathering his army, Birney emptied Baltimore's jails and slave pens. This brought howls of protest from Maryland slave-holders, some of whom had sent their slaves to pens to avoid having to commit them for military service. By the end of August, Colonel Birney had a regiment of 1,002 men in Baltimore. Two months later, when President Lincoln sent a note asking him how many blacks he had recruited, that number had grown by more than 25 percent. "Between 1,250 and 1,300, as near as I can judge," the colonel proudly replied to the president. With troops in hand, he began the arduous task of transforming his raw recruits into fighting men. He and the other officers had no illusions. Some of the men had never held or fired a weapon; most knew little about being soldiers.

There were serious concerns that former slaves, beaten and whipped into servitude for years by their masters, lacked the temperament and fortitude to be brave soldiers. Birney was not ignorant of this concern. The slave master's goal had been to cower those held as chattel, robbing them of their manhood. It was anyone's guess how the former slave would perform when called upon to fight. For now, Union leaders had to content themselves with the eagerness of blacks, slave and freeman alike, to join the battle.

Birney had just weeks to get the men ready. He began with the basics. From dusk to dawn the men drilled, learning flanking and marching maneuvers. The drills simulated the movements of troops during actual combat. The idea was to train until the movements became second nature, done without thought.

The recruits learned to march in line of battle and in a column, to march in a hollow square. They were drilled to move as a single body. They studied the drill book until they were able to perform a passage of lines in which the front of the line left gaps for rear units to move forward. They learned to deploy lines by turning the battle line like the hand of a clock to change direction on a battlefield. They learned how to "pass a defile" by converting a long horizontal line of battle into almost single file to cross a bridge or obstacle and then re-form the battle line on the other side. They learned complex wheeling motions, and how to throw out pickets as lookouts for the rest of the force.

The men were driven to near exhaustion each day. But Birney and the other officers knew that in actual combat the training would be invaluable. On the battlefield, training often made the difference between life and death.

Fleetwood and Hilton's 4th Regiment was armed with the Springfield M1861 rifled musket and the Enfield P1853 rifled musket, both popular, though increasingly outdated, weapons. These single-shot, muzzle-loading muskets were devastating at a distance of fifty yards, but effective up to two hundred yards. Their design had changed little since the 1840s, although a percussion cap was used to ignite the gunpowder rather than the antiquated piece of flint. Both were fitted with socket bayonets for hand-to-hand fighting.

The rifles fired a low-velocity minié ball, a streamlined, long-range bullet developed in 1848 by Claude Étienne Minié, a captain in the French army. The heavy minié balls were feared ammunition, leaving gaping wounds and shattered bones. Dragging germs and dirt deep into wounds, the devastating bullets were a significant cause of infection and accounted for about 90 percent of battlefield casualties during the war.

Though well drilled and dangerously armed, black recruits were constantly reminded that they were not considered the equals of their white counterparts. One glaring example was pay. While blacks trained as hard as the whites and faced similar dangers on the battlefield, they were paid less for their efforts. White privates received $13 a month, with a $3.50 clothing allowance. Blacks were paid ten dollars, with three dollars deducted for clothing. The discrepancy in pay nettled many black soldiers and was a constant subject of contention.

But the discrimination and bigotry extended well beyond pay. It existed even among the white officers in whose hands the fate of black troops was placed. First Lieutenant Samuel Watson Vannuys, a twenty-two-year-old Indiana native who had fought at Gettysburg, typified such prejudice. Vannuys, who began his service in the Union army as a private in Company F of the 7th Indiana Volunteers, initially questioned the wisdom of Lincoln's Emancipation Proclamation in a letter home, dated February 15, 1863:

"I find the boys do not approve of the proclamation generally nor of Uncle Abe's idea of arming the Negroes. They are for anything to stop the war but have not much faith in such measures accomplishing it."

In April that same year, in a letter to his parents, he raised the question of obtaining promotion by volunteering for a black regiment. "There has been a good deal of excitement among the boys of late, on the Negro question. Some of our officers propose furnishing enough volunteers from our Regt. to officer a Regt. of darkies; they have sent a petition to the Sec'y of War, and the names of those willing to take commissions. . . . I was urged to give my name for a 2nd Lieutenancy but refused for several reasons. I ant hardly an abolitionist yet to go that far. . . . What would the people of Johnson County think of a fellow who would descend so low as to command 'Niggers?'"

But with few other options for advancement, ambition softened prejudice, and Vannuys warmed to the idea of leading blacks. Service in a black regiment promised the chance to be a commissioned officer—he was intent not to go through the war as a private. He wrote another letter to his father a few weeks later acknowledging that he would be open to a position to command black soldiers.

"You say Morton and Noble offered me for a commission in an African Regt. and ask if I would be willing to accept such a position. I would prefer a white Regt. but would take a place in an African Regt. if offered."

After Gettysburg, Vannuys accepted a post in the regiment Fleetwood, Veal, and Hilton would later join. At the time he wrote home, "I received my appointment as 1st Lieutenant in the 4th Regt. U.S. Colored Troops . . . I have only been here one day. The Negro are rather dull and will require drilling to make soldiers, but not more than a company of raw whites."

Five days after Fleetwood and Hilton enlisted, Vannuys wrote in a letter, "In point of size and intelligence my company is equal to any in the regiment. I have a number who can read and write. Most are from the country and the darkies from the country are much easier to manage than the town Negro's."

In the days and months ahead, Vannuys would come to think highly of the men with whom initially he was so reluctant to serve. His metamorphosis—from open prejudice to acceptance and, finally, grudging respect—was not unusual among white officers leading black troops. His newfound faith in black soldiers would face the ultimate test at New Market Heights. That day, the young white officer who developed a close friendship with Fleetwood would be at the side of the black troops as they streamed across the open field under a hail of Confederate gunfire.

But the New Market Heights battle was still a year away on September 1, 1863, when the 4th U.S. Colored Troops completed basic training and was presented its colors in an elaborate ceremony. That day, a large group from Baltimore's black population arrived at Camp Birney bringing food and other tokens of their appreciation for the city's first black soldiers. It was a moving ceremony that reflected the bottled-up hopes and aspirations the town's black population placed in the first regiment comprised of people of their race. Blacks, they believed, were now fully engaged in the great struggle, and only good could come of it. Several impassioned speeches were made. Then the crowd gathered around the men and sang with such gusto that Vannuys, moved by the moment, described the sound as a "glorious sing."

The ladies of the city designed and produced a colorful hand-sewn regimental flag that bore the regiment's designation. This banner would become a rallying symbol in the bloody days ahead. And on that fateful day at New Market Heights, men would die to keep its colors fluttering in the wind.

THREE

THE FIRST MISSION

With basic training over, the 4th was eager to flex its muscles. But the first assignment for Fleetwood and company wasn't confronting the enemy on the battlefield. Instead, the 4th was given the inglorious job of building fortifications near Fort Monroe in Virginia.

Named after America's fifth president, James Monroe, the fort was a massive stone stronghold on the James River near the mouth of Chesapeake Bay. It sat on waterways to the Atlantic Ocean, East Coast shipping channels, and Virginia inlets stretching as far as Richmond and Petersburg.

The fort was officially manned in 1823, the same year Monroe announced his doctrine against European intervention in the New World. Eminently defensible, the fort was one of four Union fortifications in the South never to fall to the Confederates. Indeed, so secure was Fort Monroe that Lincoln felt it safe to visit during the height of the war.

It was at this dreary fort that the young artillery officer and writer Edgar Allan Poe did part of his military service in 1828.

Confederate general Robert E. Lee served as a young officer in the Army Corps of Engineers there during the early 1830s. In a twist of fate, Lee helped expand the protective moats around the fort that were so successful in keeping Confederate troops at bay during the Civil War.

By September 1863, Union major general J. G. Foster was training black troops at the fort and using them to build up nearby protections. Rebels, too, were busy in the area, and Foster again pressed Washington for long-sought reinforcements. He reported to Secretary of War Stanton on September 25 that more black troops were needed because "the white troops being much broken down by sickness." He urged that the freshly mustered 4th be "ordered down at once," especially to Yorktown, "where the regiments are very much enfeebled by sickness." Stanton received the request at 5:40 P.M. that same day, and immediately ordered the 4th to leave Baltimore. He sent Foster a message two hours later notifying him that help was on the way.

Fleetwood, Hilton, and the rest of the unit boarded a steamer and sailed south down the Chesapeake Bay to Hampton Roads, near the mouth of the James River. For ten days the 4th took part in drills and the construction of fortifications near Fort Monroe.

It was hardly what many of the soldiers envisioned when they signed up, and most itched for action. The black soldiers, Fleetwood included, found that they were far more likely than whites to be assigned to digging ditches and building fortifications. It was backbreaking, grueling work, and as the war progressed they began to openly grumble about their treatment.

On October 5, 1863, the action the troops eagerly hoped for appeared imminent. At about 5 A.M., the troops were roused in preparation for a search-and-destroy mission behind enemy lines. Their target was a highly efficient sabotage unit commonly known as the Confederate Volunteer Coast Guard. The unit, which blocked shipping channels and wreaked havoc on supply lines, ran operations along the Piankatank and North rivers.

Fleetwood grabbed his gear as the regiment lined up in the predawn darkness. With sunrise still an hour away, the troops set out along the winding Virginia roads for Mathews County, situated on a peninsula jutting into the Chesapeake Bay, some thirty miles to the north. The regiment was joined by the 11th Cavalry from Pennsylvania, the 1st New York Mounted Rifles, and artillery from the 8th New York Battery and the 1st Pennsylvania Light Artillery.

The men, untried by combat, struggled with their fears, aware that this was no drill. Fleetwood, Veal, Hilton, and the other black troops had never faced the enemy. Now there was talk up and down the ranks about the imminent possibility of seeing action against rebel soldiers. They had trained for this moment, but the realization of it brought a mixture of excitement and dread.

For Fleetwood, the heavily wooded hillsides of rural Virginia stood in stark contrast to the urban landscape of his hometown, Baltimore. But he knew the tranquillity was deceiving, for every treed hillside and wooded knoll held the possibility of ambush. He steeled his jangling nerves, determined to be courageous no matter what danger lay ahead. Others in the 744-strong regiment seemed similarly resolved. As if they had something to prove, the men marched ramrod straight in strict file as when on parade, with few stragglers.

Brigadier General Isaac J. Wistar, a wily, daring veteran of several battles, headed the expedition. His résumé was impressive. He had led regiments at Fair Oaks, Savage's Station,

Charles City Station, Malvern Hill, and other skirmishes. He fought in the Second Bull Run and was wounded at Antietam, scene of the single deadliest day of fighting in the Civil War.

Wistar was uneasy about marching with raw recruits, especially black soldiers, whom he eyed closely with suspicion. He knew that the success of his mission rested in part on the shoulders of untried men, some of whom as recently as months earlier bore the shackles of slavery. It was a discomforting realization.

Union officers were uncertain just how many rebels were operating in the area. But judging from their past success, it was clear that the Confederates were seasoned fighters who knew the terrain well. Wistar needed an edge. His plan was to limit the movement of the enemy by shutting down traffic on water and land. To be effective, he and his troops had to move quickly.

Wistar sent U.S. Navy gunboats up the Piankatank and North rivers to prevent the rebels from escaping by water. Then he ordered his cavalry units to race ahead of the foot soldiers to the Gloucester Court House with the best mounted squadrons. They were to seize all the roads leading down into Mathews County and hold them, detaining all passengers.

Fleetwood, Hilton, and the rest of the 4th marched throughout the autumn day. It was difficult going. They arrived at the neck of Mathews County at dusk, where they were ordered on reconnaissance detail. It had been a hard ten-hour march. Legs ached with exhaustion, and feet were blistered. But they set out to explore the area. It was beautiful country. Open fields of oats abutted rows of corn, ready to be picked and shucked. Sheep, chickens, and cattle were in abundance. But the soldiers were under strict orders not to pilfer or enter any of the homes in the area.

Wistar ordered the black regiment to set up a quick camp

between the two rivers where the major roads in the county converged. The cavalry units remained stationed at the routes leading out of the peninsula. This effectively closed all traffic in and out the area. Wistar set up his headquarters near the infantry and surrounded the regiments with guards to warn of oncoming rebel soldiers.

That night, an uneasy Fleetwood and his fellow soldiers slept on open ground. No one knew what to expect. The men had no idea if Confederate troops were gathered over the next ridge ready to attack, or were fifty miles down the road. Some of the regiment stayed up all night worried that the enemy could suddenly appear.

The soldiers were stirred at about 4:30 A.M. with no rebel troops in sight. At daylight, the cavalry units began a thorough examination of the area. The troops were instructed to explore every nook, corner, creek, and landing place. They remained on the highest alert, but the anticipated pitched battle with the wily enemy never materialized. However, the massive search was not completely in vain. The soldiers still found plenty: livestock, boats, weapons, and rebel sympathizers.

The tally was impressive. The troops destroyed 130 boats and sloops, the kind used to terrorize the Union navy. They rounded up and captured eighty head of beef cattle belonging to the Confederate government and en route to Richmond. A few horses and small arms were taken. They arrested about a hundred people involved in illicit trade with the South.

Just when it seemed the operation would progress without casualties, a single shot, followed by a sharp cry and shouts, jarred the soldiers into action. The men rushed to the sound of the gunshot and discovered the body of a fallen comrade, shot from ambush. His killer, a backwoodsman named Smith, was caught almost immediately.

Wistar ordered an immediate drumhead court-martial. Troops in the vicinity of the shooting claimed they saw the man kill the soldier. Wistar didn't hesitate in issuing judgment. He ordered Smith hanged on the spot. Within minutes, Smith was hoisted up, his legs kicking futilely as his body desperately sought the air being denied by an ever-tightening noose. It was a brutal, ugly death, especially for those in the regiment who had never witnessed a hanging. Soon, Smith's lifeless body swung grotesquely in the autumn air, a reminder, as if one were needed, of the viciousness of war.

By October 9—five days after the operation began—the 4th was marching back on the long, thirty-mile hike to Fort Monroe. Fleetwood, Veal, and Hilton, as well as the officers in the newly formed regiment, took a special pride in the success of their mission. The men had no illusions. There had been no pitched battles, no moments of heroism. But they did everything they were asked and no one had deserted. Despite their short training and sparse experience, they had performed like veterans.

Vannuys still harbored misgivings about the blacks troops, but was impressed with their performance. "We got into camp last night at about 10 o'clock—marched 25 miles," the young officer wrote in a letter home. "[The black troops] stood the march very well. Better I believe than any Regt. I ever saw."

Wistar, the experienced veteran, was also impressed and pleasantly surprised. "The Negro infantry marched better than any old troops I ever saw," he wrote in an official report. "On two days they marched 30 miles a day without a straggler or a complaint, and were ready for picket, patrol, or detachment duty at night. Not a fence rail was burned or a chicken stolen by them. They seem to be well controlled and their discipline, obedience, and cheerfulness, for new troops, are surprising, and have dispelled many of my prejudices."

But the blacks hadn't joined the army to march or prove they wouldn't steal chickens. And the compliments, though welcomed, only served to harden their resolve to see action.

FOUR

READY AND WILLING
The Cincinnati Brigade

Powhatan Beaty arrived at the recruiting station at Camp Delaware, Ohio, on June 17, 1863, two weeks before the fighting at Gettysburg began. He had come to fight for the Union and, more importantly, its cause. Camp Delaware, on the east bank of the winding Olentangy River, was a makeshift recruitment and training center set up that spring for Ohio's black enlistees. Across the murky, slow-moving river, a better-appointed camp trained white recruits.

The camp was created with the blessing of Ohio governor David Tod, who initially opposed the enlistment of blacks but later saw it as a way to ease some of the dissatisfaction within the white community over the draft. It was one of the great ironies of Ohio politics that in a state where blacks could only dream of equality, black recruits counted equal with whites in filling the state's quota for soldiers.

At twenty-four, Powhatan Beaty was already a veteran, having served nine months earlier in an all-black brigade hastily put together to help defend Cincinnati. But the city wasn't attacked and Beaty saw no action. Now the wiry, five-foot-seven-inch farmer with intense, smoldering eyes and a lean, angular face framed by long black hair was prepared to serve again.

This enlistment would be different. He would see his share of bloodshed, and long before the war ended Beaty would join Christian Fleetwood and a band of battle-weary black soldiers on a killing field in the southern woodlands of Virginia.

Beaty understood the importance to his race of the North's winning the war. In June 1863, following a string of Union defeats, that prospect was very much in doubt.

Almost immediately upon enlisting for three years in a regiment that would become known as the 5th U.S. Colored Infantry, Beaty was promoted to sergeant, the highest rank a black could attain in the Union forces. It was a far cry from his first stint of military service.

Nine months earlier, although willing and eager to fight, Beaty and hundreds of other blacks in Cincinnati had suffered the indignity of being impressed into military service at the end of bayonets and billy clubs. They were among the first black troops in the Union during the Civil War. As a testament to their novelty, they were simply called "The Black Brigade." But their pride at being first was tempered by deep resentment over how the brigade was created.

After the fall of Federal forces at Richmond, Kentucky, on August 30, 1862, Cincinnati, a hundred miles to the north, was wide open to attack by rebel soldiers. No organized troops stood between the city and the rebels. Confederate general Edmund Kirby Smith was marching north through Kentucky with four divisions totaling twenty-one thousand battle-proven men. After his victory at Richmond, he turned his eyes to Cincinnati, on the southern border of Ohio. Also eyeing the city was Confederate raider and renegade Kentuckian John Morgan, whose band of irregulars were feared for their fierce, daring attacks.

In Richmond, the Confederates quickly overpowered Federal forces, killing or capturing more than four thousand Union troops in a decisive two-day battle. Now panic swept Cincinnati as the Confederate troops appeared headed for the city. "To Arms," cried the *Cincinnati Gazette*. "The time for playing war has passed. The enemy is now approaching our doors."

Their city in jeopardy, Beaty and his fellow blacks were willing to fight. But they seriously doubted they would be allowed to, especially in a city where racial oppression reached lawless and epidemic proportions. Just a month before the fall of Richmond, several blacks were killed or injured in racially driven mob violence in Cincinnati.

It was a turbulent, ugly time when "colored men of the North were everywhere contemptuously refused permission to participate in the great struggle which is opening the prison-doors up to their brethren in the South," wrote Peter Clarke, a black resident of Cincinnati. "In no community was this exclusion more generally ratified by public sentiment than in Cincinnati."

Those who knew the underpinnings of the city weren't surprised by Clarke's assertions. Cincinnati, on the banks of the Ohio River, was a bustling, hog-slaughtering, meatpacking town of 161,000, whose commercial relationships reached as far north as its sympathies lay south. Most of Ohio was firmly pledged to the Union. But Cincinnati, which shared a river border with the pro-Union, slave-owning state of Kentucky, had more in common with the perspective below the Mason-Dixon Line.

Like a great equivocator, the city seemed unable to decide where it stood on slavery. City leaders accommodated their antislavery Northern customers by allowing free speech about the evils of slavery. Yet pro-slavers and abolitionists regularly vied for space or stood side by side in the marketplace, competing for the attention of curious passersby.

It made for colorful, if unpredictable, theater. A speaker railing against the Union spoke to a packed house without interruption that year, while a pro-Union speaker was driven from the same platform by angry supporters of slavery. Halls were closed to stop a lecture by famed abolitionist clergyman and orator Henry Ward Beecher because authorities thought it would provoke a riot. Beecher was the brother of Harriet Beecher Stowe, author of the controversial 1852 best-seller *Uncle Tom's Cabin*, a scathing indictment of the ills of slavery that inadvertently gave America one of its most enduring racial stereotypes. Stowe's book so angered pro-slavers and galvanized abolitionists into action that President Lincoln once half-jokingly told her that she helped start the Civil War.

In Cincinnati, a city where mob violence against blacks was often permitted and indulged in by the police, Beecher's presence was deemed the spark that could ignite the ever-simmering racial powder keg. Racial tension was nothing new in Cincinnati, the site of reoccurring violence against its free black residents dating back decades. These attacks often resulted in the destruction of black-owned property and even murder.

Now, with the double threat from the Confederate army and renegade raider John Morgan growing daily, city leaders called for a united front against the enemy. On September 1, 1862, the city began raising regiments to defend against the Confederates. The impending attack, like an unchecked wildfire or great gathering storm, grew more threatening by the hour. There was a tangible air of martial fervor, yet blacks made little effort to join in the organized defense of Cincinnati. Experience had taught them that they were not welcomed by city leaders.

Peter Clarke, fully aware of the dilemma of his fellow black

Cincinnatians, noted that there was an "ellipsis" universal in American thought and speech at the time. "When an American writes, 'All men are created free and equal,' he means all white men. When he solicits the patron-age of the public for his book, his lecture, his concert, his store, his railroad-car or steamboat, he means the white public."

Beaty and other black residents were bitterly reminded of this at the outset of the war. During the rush to enlist after the attack on Fort Sumter, black residents in Cincinnati held a meeting to organize a "home guard" among their ranks. They desperately wanted to fight the Confederates, with the hope that their efforts and a Union victory would spell liberty for slaves and advancement for free blacks.

But the thought of an army of black residents alarmed many in the city. The Cincinnati police swooped in and demanded the keys to the schoolhouse where the group met. The owner of a shop who had offered to turn his building into a recruiting station was ordered to take down an American flag he had raised over the door.

The idea of blacks killing whites—even during a war—was abhorrent to many white residents of Cincinnati. The oft-repeated message was that this was a white man's war and that "niggers" need not apply.

This rebuke stung deeply.

"The blood boils with indignation at the remembrance of the insults heaped upon them for this simple offer," Clarke wrote of black feelings over how the authorities dealt with their attempt to form a home guard. Now, with rebel soldiers approaching their city, Powhatan Beaty and other black residents recalled their earlier attempt to volunteer and were unwilling to make the same mistake twice. They decided to wait and watch.

That decision would cause blacks great grief.

On September 1, Union general Lewis Wallace assumed command of Cincinnati, placing it under martial law. He immediately issued a call for troops. His proclamation, published in the local newspapers, stated, "This labor ought to be that of love. The undersigned trusts and believes it will be so. Anyhow, it must be done. The willing shall be properly credited; the unwilling promptly visited."

The next day, with an attack on his city looming, Cincinnati mayor George Hatch, a man whose racial bigotry was deep felt, well documented, and publicly enunciated, issued a desperate call in local evening newspapers for businesses to close at 10 A.M. the following day and all the city's residents to gather "in their respective wards, at the usual places of voting, and then and there organize themselves in such manner as may be thought best for the defense of the city. Every man, of every age, be he citizen or alien, who lives under the protection of our laws, is expected to take part in the organization."

On the surface, the mayor's proclamation appeared explicit enough and seemed to include blacks: "Every man, of every age, be he citizen or alien." But the mayor's request that residents assemble at their usual voting places was confusing. Blacks weren't allowed to vote. And after all, Mayor Hatch was the man who broke up the movement for a black home guard. Thus, many blacks doubted that the order included them.

The Cincinnati police, who had been empowered by Hatch to round up citizens for General Wallace, made it clear that blacks weren't welcomed. When a black resident asked an officer if the mayor expected blacks to report for duty, he was strongly rebuffed. "You know damned well he doesn't mean you," the policeman snapped. "Niggers ain't citizens."

"But he calls on all citizens and aliens," came the retort. "If he does not mean all, he should not say so."

"The mayor knows as well as you do what to write, and all he wants is for you niggers to keep quiet."

But Union officials weren't so quick to dismiss help from black residents. Unaware of the depth of racial tensions in the city, General Wallace was surprised that so few blacks came forward, and he sent the police to round up black men for duty. Many of them would have volunteered, if asked. Instead, they were subjected to the brutality of the Cincinnati police, some of whom had actively participated in the mob violence against the black community just a month earlier.

Blacks were dragged from the fields, their jobs, and their homes. The police went from house to house, breaking down doors and ordering men at the point of bayonets into the streets. The authorities searched closets and cellars, thrusting bayonets into beds and bedding. The young and old, in varying stages of agitation, dress, and infirmity, were herded into the streets amid shouts and jeers. Gangs of boys, yelling profanities and insults, followed the police as they marched the men through town toward an old mule pen. Stripped of their dignity, they were paraded like criminals along Plum Street, past the grand cathedral, every man branded a coward in the eyes of the jeering public.

Blacks seethed with anger but were powerless. This was the story of their lives, to be relegated by color to a status that had no currency in their society. In name they were free men; in reality they lived within boundaries set by those who viewed themselves as their superiors and regarded them with disdain, disgust, and great contempt.

Beaty and others were marched off into the night without being told where they were being taken, their wives, children, and relatives left to wonder if they would ever see them again. "We were torn from our homes, from the streets, from our shops, and driven to the mule-pen on Plum Street at the point of the bayonet, without any definite knowledge of what we were wanted for," recalled Marshall P. H. Jones, a victim of the roundup.

They would soon learn. For even in the face of great danger their white fellow citizens had no intention of allowing blacks to fight to protect their loved ones and homes. Beaty and other blacks were to be conscripts of the lowest rank, laborers and ditchdiggers, performing tasks few whites wanted to do.

The ill-treatment of blacks was ignored by all but one local newspaper the next morning. The *Cincinnati Gazette*'s Thursday edition pleaded, "Let our colored fellow soldiers be treated civilly, and not exposed to any unnecessary tyranny, nor to the insults of poor whites. We say poor whites for none but poor spirited whites insult a race which they profess to regard as inferior. It would have been decent to have invited the colored inhabitants to turn out in defense of the city. Then there would have been an opportunity to compare their patriotism with that of those who were recently trying to drive them from the city. Since the services of men are required from our colored brethren, let them be treated like men."

By September 20, the threat of invasion had passed. The Confederates shifted their forces elsewhere, and the siege of Cincinnati was over. The Black Brigade was immediately disbanded. Few could blame Beaty and his fellow black Cincinnatians if they wanted nothing more to do with the war. They had been herded like wild animals and subjected to public ridicule and abuse.

Yet when the Union extended an invitation to rejoin the war effort, Beaty and others willingly enlisted. Some became members of the 54th U.S. Volunteers, and would die in the siege of Fort Wagner. Others would enlist in Mississippi and fight on its banks. Some would fight and die on Morris Island.

Others, continuing in that proud tradition, joined Beaty at Camp Delaware—men like James H. Bronson, Robert Pinn, and Milton M. Holland, all of whom would do battle at New Market Heights.

Bronson was a twenty-five-year-old barber from Delaware County when he enlisted on Independence Day. He was promoted to first sergeant less than two months later. The strapping, six-foot Pinn was a twenty-year-old farmer from Cincinnati when he showed up at Camp Delaware on September 5. He was promoted to sergeant on October 18.

Of the three, nineteen-year-old Milton Holland had the greatest understanding of the impact of slavery and the importance of the war. He was born a slave in Texas in 1844. The man believed to be his father, Bird Holland, owned him, his mother, and his two brothers. But the white blood coursing through his veins offered no protection from enslavement. He would remain a slave until his father decided to marry a white woman in the late 1850s, at which time he and his brothers were granted their freedom and sent to Ohio.

Bird Holland, briefly secretary of state in Texas in 1861, died while serving in the Confederate army. The son he likely fathered by a slave—a broad-shouldered Texan with strong, chiseled features and a tight smile—would win praise fighting that army. In a way it was a summation of the war: a white father fighting to preserve the "peculiar institution" that elevated him to the status of master, pitted against his illegitimate black son desperate to destroy the institution that once made him the property of another.

Such was the nature of the great war. For blacks like Holland, Beaty, Bronson, and Pinn, a Union victory was the only acceptable outcome. They knew it was not melodramatic to state that the very future of their race depended on it.

FIVE

HUNTING GUERRILLAS AND BUSHWHACKERS IN NORTH CAROLINA

In the autumn of 1863, as the Union was resupplying its ranks with new recruits, Lee's army was safely back in southern Virginia, preparing for winter. General Meade's pursuit of the Confederate army had stalled, leaving Lincoln with shaken confidence in his commander. No end to the war appeared in sight.

Lee's retreat created a state of lawlessness in the swampy valleys of North Carolina, where roving bands of rebel guerrillas operated across ever-shifting battlefields. These raiding parties specialized in hit-and-run attacks against Federal expeditions, often setting up blockades of canals that served Union supply lines. While not officially part of the Confederate army, the groups were often sponsored and supplied by the state as militia units. In addition, bushwhackers, generally backwoodsmen with Southern allegiance, took advantage of the general lack of security to pillage pro-Union towns under the pretense of fighting for the Confederate cause.

General Butler, who was now in charge of operations in

Virginia where the black regiments were stationed, saw no distinction between bushwhacker and raider. He viewed them all as pillagers, pirates, and terrorists. Tiring of attacks by these shadowy fighters, he decided to rid the region of these nettlesome Southern sympathizers.

In December, Butler ordered Major General Edward Wild, the controversial commander whose exploits lived up to his name, to take two black regiments into North Carolina for a three-week expedition with the explicit permission to use whatever means necessary to clear the area of raiders. It was a sweeping mandate in an unconventional war against an unconventional enemy.

Wild was just the man for the job.

If Butler was a beast, Wild was a terror. Hard, driven, and unyielding, his tactics sometimes drove even Union-leaning residents to join the other side. He was a daring, inspiring figure in battle, and black troops felt fortunate he led their ranks. He had lost an arm at the battle of Antietam, a fact he treated as a mere inconvenience.

Wild's passion for battle was in no way diminished by the loss of an appendage, even one as useful as an arm. He would ride at the head of his regiment, pistol in hand, cheering his soldiers to victory. Milton Holland called Wild "a noble and brave man . . . the right man in the right place." It was a gushing sentiment echoed among the troops.

Before the war, Wild had been a noted physician. After Harvard Medical School, he gave medical lectures in Paris, and later served as a medical officer in the Turkish army during the Crimean War. When fighting broke out in America, he was commissioned as a captain. He fought in the First Bull Run and during the Peninsula Campaign, and was wounded at Fair Oaks. He left the service in July 1862, but the sedentary life of retirement didn't sit well with him. One-armed or not, he lived for the heat of battle. His chance to again lead men into combat came with the creation of black regiments.

The previous April, the War Department had authorized Wild to raise a black regiment. He did so in enemy territory. A Confederate dispatch dated June 9 noted that Cavalry general A. P. Hill had learned that General Wild was in New Bern, North Carolina, raising a regiment of black troops. It was a nightmare scenario for Confederate leaders: subjugated blacks being trained and armed to fight for their own freedom.

Wild was now back in northern Virginia, seeking recruits from slaves crossing the lines for his 2nd North Carolina Volunteers. The black infantry unit was later renamed the 36th U.S. Colored Infantry.

Wild was also attracting free blacks. James Gardiner, who would go on to fight at New Market Heights, was one such recruit. The nineteen-year-old oysterman, who enlisted as a private on September 15 when Wild's troops came to Gloucester, had never known the shackles of slavery, but hated the institution as deeply as any man. He enlisted because he believed he had a moral obligation to do so. Also enlisted in Wild's unit was future New Market Heights combatant Miles James, who joined that year in Norfolk.

Recruits in hand and hastily trained, Wild set out on his mission.

On Saturday, December 5, the 2nd North Carolina Volunteers began the grueling march to North Carolina. They would have plenty of help on this expedition. Members of the 5th and 1st Colored Troops regiments were also on the way to join them.

Powhatan Beaty, James Bronson, Milton Holland, and Robert Pinn were among 530 soldiers from the 5th who left their camps northeast of Norfolk. They marched past

Kempsville, Great Bridge, and the Northwest Landing to South Mills.

Meanwhile, Gardiner and James were among the four hundred soldiers of the 2nd North Carolina Colored Volunteers marching from their camp outside of Portsmouth. They headed for Deep Creek and the Dismal Swamp Canal accompanied by seven hundred troops from the 1st. Altogether more than sixteen hundred black soldiers embarked on the mission into enemy territory to capture or destroy the elusive guerrillas whose reign of terror had made life miserable for soldier and civilian alike.

Two small steamers loaded with rations for the troops were to meet up with them farther down the canal. But a navigating blunder sent the boats down the wrong waterway. The 5th waited for the steamers at South Mills. When it was apparent the boats weren't coming, Wild sent messengers to the captains of the steamers to meet them at Elizabeth City. The hungry troops were sent out to confiscate food and supplies. They targeted the most pro-Southern residents in the area, taking what they needed but with strict orders not to loot. They continued to forage as they marched to the Camden Court House and back to South Mills, where the two columns met up and were reinforced by two regiments from Pennsylvania.

Wild wanted his troops to move back and forth freely over the Pasquotank River, below South Mills. To do so, they needed a bridge. But there was no lumber. That problem was solved by stripping planks from a nearby house and barn belonging to a Confederate captain. The buildings yielded enough lumber for a substantial bridge, and the soldiers had no qualms about depriving an enemy officer of his abode.

With the bridge erected, the troops crossed the river and marched to Elizabeth City, where they headquartered for the next week, camping in the chilly December air. They were hardly idle. Patrols were sent out to locate and hunt down the guerrillas. Other troops were detailed to rustle up food and fire-wood, both of which were in scarce supply and badly needed. Everyone was instructed to encourage any escaped slaves they encountered to join the regiment.

The steamers finally arrived, and the men were put to work unloading the boats. Wild then sent the steamers to tow schooners back and forth from Roanoke Island with loads of black families and their belongings headed north. Soon, a small exodus was under way.

But the enemy, too, had been busy. Patrols reported that the hastily constructed bridge was burned out and all communications cut off. So far, the guerrillas had avoided Union forces. That was about to change.

That night, as soldiers huddled near campfires for warmth, guerrillas launched a surprise attack, shooting several volleys at the camp before melting away into the darkness. There were no casualties, but the rattled soldiers now had a greater sense of vulnerability.

The next day, soldiers fanned out and scoured the surrounding woods looking for the attackers. The troops tried unsuccessfully to trap the enemy, but the rebels knew the area too well and easily avoided capture. They had simply vanished; so too had two black soldiers.

One of the missing men was from the 36th. The cavalry unit found him hanging from a tree, a note pinned to his cold flesh as a final indignity. Holland, Bronson, Beaty, and Pinn had trained with him. Now they helped bury him.

The note was an exclamation mark to a brutal murder, clearly meant as a warning to other black soldiers. No one doubted they would meet a similar fate if captured by the rebels. But the men who killed the soldier didn't know the mettle of the men they faced. It was anger and a burning desire for revenge, not fear, that settled on the troops. Holland captured the collective fury of his fellow black soldiers when he promised that the killers would not go unpunished. "Before this war ends we will pin their sentences to them with Uncle Sam's leaden pills." Those who knew the outspoken Texan realized it was hardly an idle threat.

The news of the soldier's killing hit Wild hard, changing the tenor of the mission. He now worried about the treatment of the remaining black soldier still held prisoner. These men were under his command, and ultimately he was responsible for their safety.

He understood the factors at play. This was a different type of warfare. Guerrillas were terrorists who didn't take prisoners. This was especially true in the case of captured black troops, who would likely be hanged or shot. Wild knew he had to send an unequivocal, powerful message that such treatment would not be tolerated. But the guerrillas had a distinct advantage. They were well supported in the surrounding areas and knew the terrain far better than the black troops. Wild was about to level the playing field.

The rebels, he knew, depended heavily on help from residents in the surrounding valleys. Wild wanted to exact a heavy price for such support to discourage further aid. To win the fight, the troops had to wage war not just on the guerrillas, but on anyone offering them haven and succor. Under Wild's new military paradigm, Union allegiances afforded a veil of protection, but Southern sympathy brought harsh retribution.

Wild later explained his strategy:

"Finding ordinary measures of little avail, I adopted a more rigorous style of warfare. [We] burned their houses and barns, ate up their livestock, and took hostages from their families.

This course we followed throughout the trip, and we learned that they were disgusted with such unexpected treatment; it bred disaffection, some wishing to quit the business, others going over the lines to join the Confederate Army."

Wild was determined to take one life for every one taken from his men. He ordered that the family of a known rebel be taken hostage. "We hold one of their 'fair daughters,' as they term them, for the good behavior of her husband, who is a guerrilla officer, toward our beloved soldiers," Holland wrote, obviously pleased with the new policy.

Implicit in Wild's actions was the assertion that the lives of his black troops were as valuable as those of whites. It was a concept so foreign to Southern sensibilities that it might as well have been developed on another planet. To Holland and other black troops long accustomed to being held in low regard by whites, the policy was a welcome indication that their commanding officer did not hold their lives lightly. This served to strengthen the resolve even of those grown tired of the war.

Wild formalized his policy in letters to two of the captains of guerrilla divisions:

Captain of Guerrillas,

Sir,

I still hold in custody, Mrs. Munden and Mrs. Weeks, as hostages for the colored soldier taken by you. As he is treated so shall they be, even to hanging. By this time you know that I am in earnest. Guerrillas are to be treated as pirates. You will never have rest until you renounce your present course or join the regular Confederate Army.

The letter was followed by aggressive military action.

In a region where armed black men were cause for alarm, the sight of black troops burning the countryside was the ultimate nightmare. The 1st U.S. Colored Troops swarmed the area, engaging the enemy in firefights. They burned two guerrilla campsites, forcing the raiders to flee. The regiment burned two more camps between Elizabeth and Hertford, taking guns, horses, provisions, clothing, and prisoners.

Wild ordered a hasty trial of one of the captured rebels, Daniel Bright. The man was quickly convicted and summarily sentenced to death. Bright, a Pasquotank County native, was hanged that day. A card attached to his body read: "This guerrilla hanged by order of Brigadier-General Wild."

After a week of inflicting damage on the guerrillas and their sympathizers, Wild moved his men out of Elizabeth City. He sent 250 soldiers to land on Powell's Point and ferried another 400 across to Camden Court House. The rest returned to South Mills. He dismissed the cavalry and artillery units, and made the 1st U.S. Colored Infantry march as a protective force with the trains of black refugees fleeing the South.

There was something almost biblical about the exodus of Southern slaves that a deeply religious soldier like Fleetwood, had he been there, would have found hard to ignore. And as the former slaves streamed north, their belongings strapped to their backs or held close in tight bundles, Fleetwood would have felt some sadness. For he knew the freedom offered the black man in the North came with caveats and conditions, not milk and honey.

Despite their success against the guerrillas, the work of the black troops in the area was hardly over. The enemy was on the run, not completely routed. Wild sent Colonel Alonzo Draper, a twenty-seven-year-old former editor and civil servant from Vermont, and about two hundred men—including Gardiner,

James, Holland, and Beaty—to probe around Shiloh, an area of known guerrilla activity. There, guerrillas mounted a sneak attack after dark on Draper's troops, firing volley after volley toward the light of the campfires. The attack could have proved deadly, but the troops escaped unscathed. Colonel Draper, anticipating subterfuge by the rebels, left the campfires burning and withdrew his men to a nearby church. Roused by the gunfire, the troops rushed into action. But the soldiers on guard duty had driven off the enemy before the Draper and his men could reach them.

The black soldiers were attacked again on Friday, December 18, at Sandy Swamp, near Indiantown, North Carolina. At about 11 A.M., as the troops marched over the Indiantown Bridge, the rear guard holding the bridge came under fire. The guerrillas were driven off after a brief fight, and a message was sent to the main column warning of rebel activity in the area.

The troops had barely gotten the warning when a volley was fired from a dense thicket of pines about four hundred yards away. Two men were killed and two seriously wounded in the ambush. Caught in the open, the soldiers dropped to the ground just as a second volley thundered, sending balls flying over their heads. They quickly returned fire and soon the air was thick with smoke, dust, and the sound of musket fire.

The troops, flat on their stomachs in the dirt, were in the open, while the enemy fired from the cover of a heavily wooded area. To stay where they were would be disastrous. The men had trained for such situations and quickly devised a counterattack even as guerrilla sharpshooters tried to keep them pinned down.

Two companies, Holland with one of them, were split off from the main column as the soldiers moved to outflank the enemy on the left and right. Anticipating close-quarter combat, the men were instructed to affix their bayonets. The remaining soldiers prepared to charge from the front once given the signal.

Holland glanced at the men around him to gauge their composure. None hesitated, though they all knew the danger. The enemy had the benefit of operating from the protective cover of the trees; the Union soldiers would have to charge from the open. Some were likely to get shot, maybe killed. With snipers' bullets whizzing by, the men calmly prepared to rush the woods.

At the signal, they sprang forward with a wild yell and blazing guns. Holland later recalled the moment with great pride. "The men stood nobly and faced the cowardly foe when they were hid in the swamp firing upon them," he noted. "They stood like men, and when ordered to charge, went in with a yell, and came out victorious, losing four killed and several wounded. The rebel loss is large, as compared with ours."

Holland and his company chased the guerrillas through the swamp. Many escaped, but not before thirteen were killed or wounded. Union casualties were eleven. It was an impressive victory, especially because the guerrillas fought from cover and still suffered greater casualties.

Holland was pleased that his unit "played her part admirably in the charge." He wasn't the only one. The officers were also impressed with the poise of the black troops under fire.

But Wild wasn't finished with the guerrillas. When Draper's troops met up with the main force at Indiantown, Wild decided to turn back with a combined force and hunt down those guerrillas who had escaped. He was intent on finishing the job.

The soldiers were sent to attack a major guerrilla camp on Knot Island in the heart of a swamp, set up by a guerrilla leader named Burroughs as a base for attacking Federal troops and interests. Since the camp was accessible only by single file over a pathway of felled trunks about half a mile long, any attempt to cross onto the island would leave soldiers dangerously exposed to an ambush or sniper fire.

The soldiers were aware of the danger but again showed no hesitation when they approached the makeshift bridge. They had tasted battle, lost comrades, and now were bent on ferreting out the enemy no matter how deep the hole into which he had crawled. They were prepared to neither give nor ask for quarter. Once on the island, the troops surrounded the guerrillas' camp, which Wild called the enemy's "citadel." In the ensuing fight, Burroughs and several of his guerrillas were captured. Others fled into the swamp, leaving guns and equipment behind, including brand-new Enfields and ammunition. The soldiers also confiscated provisions, rebel uniforms, and shoes. After setting fire to the camp, they chased the fleeing guerrillas, burning the houses of several rebel sympathizers they encountered along the way.

Such action was having the desired affect of chilling support for the rebels. The troops talked with residents and found many sick of war. Those who sympathized with the South were caught up in their own troubles, having been plundered and looted by both sides. Some felt it was a lost cause and believed slavery was doomed. "They were aware of the mischief arising from the presence of guerrillas in their midst," noted Wild. "If really neutral, or sympathizing with the North, they were usually, and reasonably, afraid to speak their minds on account of guerrillas. But the rapid development of loyal sentiment as we progressed with our raid was really surprising, if not comforting."

On December 21, a day after the final conflict in the swamp, the troops began their march homeward. They brought with them black refugees and rebel prisoners, who, along with the wounded, sick, and lame, were loaded aboard the steamer. The troops moved at the impressive clip of more than twenty-five miles a day, arriving back at camp on Christmas Eve day. Holland was exhilarated by the experience of their first expedition. "I must say of the 5th, that after twenty days of hard scouting, without overcoats or blankets, they returned home to camp, which the soldiers term their home, making twenty-five and thirty miles per day. Several of [the] white cavalry told me that no soldiers have ever done as hard marching through swamps and marshes as cheerfully as we did, and that if they had to follow us for any length of time it would kill their horses. During that raid, thousands of slaves belonging to rebel masters were liberated. You are aware that the colored man makes no distinction in regard to persons, so I may say all belonging to slaveholders were liberated."

Expeditions are often measured by a variety of standards. By any account this one was a success. From a military perspective, it had netted nine boatloads of booty placed onto steamers at Roanoke Island and another four trains of goods overland. About twenty-five hundred slaves were freed. Four guerrilla camps were burned, along with more than a dozen rebel-owned homesteads and two distilleries. The soldiers captured more than fifty guns and took dozens of prisoners, including six Confederate soldiers on furloughs. They confiscated four large boats used in contraband trade as well as several horses.

At the same time, the Union losses were relatively light. Seven of Wild's troops were killed, nine wounded, and two captured by the enemy. One man died of poison, three of disease, and several others were taken ill by fatigue or exposure to smallpox and the mumps.

From the perspective of the black troops, the expedition was an unmitigated success. They had fought bravely, proven themselves in the heat of combat. They knew their performance was under a microscope, part of the "Negro experiment" now taking place with black troops all over the country. But in their willingness to sacrifice their lives they sought higher dividends than wages. They sought respect.

Holland's letter home reflected that craving:

"The boys are generally well, and satisfied that though they are deprived of all the comforts of home, and laboring under great disadvantages as regards pay and having families to support upon less wages than white soldiers, still trust that when they do return they will be crowned with honors, and a happier home prepared for them, when they will be free from the abuses of northern and southern fire-eaters. Though we should fall struggling in our blood for right and justice, for the freedom of our brothers in bondage, or fall in defense of our national color, the Stars and Stripes, our home and fireside will ever be protected by our old friend Gov. [David] Tod, by the loyalty of Abraham Lincoln, our Moses, and the all-wise God that created us. Friends at home be cheerful, cast aside all mercenary compensation. Spring forth to the call and show to the world that you are men. You have thus far shown, and still continue to show yourselves worthy of freedom, and you will win the respect of the whole nation. There is a brighter day coming for the colored man, and he must sacrifice home comforts if necessary to speed the coming of that glorious day. I will close my letter in the language of the immortal Henry 'Give me liberty, or give me death!'"

Indeed, much of the country was watching. When the debate in New York raged over whether to raise black troops the following spring, authorities sent inquires asking residents how black troops performed during the expedition. Thomas Jackson, superintendent of the First Sub-District of Virginia, responded: "In reply to your inquiry as to the proved capacity of colored men as soldiers, I can only, so far as field service, give the testimony of those who have had opportunities of seeing them on the march and in presence of the enemy. There, all agree that as soldiers, colored men come fully up to the expectations of their warmest friends."

Jackson particularly remembered the black troops led by Colonel Draper. "Col. Draper, did more to break up roving bands of rebels in this district, than any regiment of white troops—not the least notable of its exploits being the capture of Burroughs, the guerrilla, at his chosen place of safety on Knot Island. During this expedition, and on subsequent scouts, as far as Currituck Court-House, nothing could be better than their endurance in marching and rapidity of movement."

In his report of the expedition, Wild praised their performance. "The men marched wonderfully, never grumbled, were watchful on picket, and always ready for fight. They are most reliable soldiers."

But the black soldiers had hardly won universal acceptance. Even after the obvious success of the expedition, Butler told Secretary of War Stanton that many white soldiers still wanted the black troops to fail. "I find between some of the officers in this department in command of white soldiers, a considerable degree of prejudice against the colored troops, and in some cases impediments have been thrown in the way of their recruiting, and they interfered with on their expeditions."

Butler promised to address the problem, which proved more entrenched and systemic than he believed. The performance of blacks in the war would continue to strengthen his case. But the black troops weren't getting any breaks; certainly not from the enemy who hated their race, and sadly not from many of their white fellow soldiers whose cause they shared.

But as 1863 ended, Christian Fleetwood marveled at the changes the year had brought. Instead of the far-off African shores of Liberia, he was in the raw winter chill of Virginia. He found it almost unbelievable that he now marched in the blue uniform of a Union soldier. More impressively, that uniform carried the stripes of a sergeant major. On the eve of the New Year, he sat down to jot his swirling thoughts in his diary.

"This year has brought about many changes that at the beginning were or would have been thought impossible," he penned. "The close of the year finds me a soldier for the cause of my race. May God bless the cause, and enable me in the coming year to forward on it."

He would need that blessing.

SIX

EARLY SKIRMISHES
Raids on Richmond

Christian Fleetwood and his regiment celebrated New Year's Day 1864 encamped near Fort Keyes, Virginia, desperately trying to keep warm in the subzero temperatures that had enveloped the East Coast and reached as far south as Memphis. The 4th, 5th, and 6th Colored regiments were stationed together, under Colonel Samuel A. Duncan.

Bored, cold, and badly in need of a new coat, Fleetwood frittered away the first part of the day finishing monthly reports and mending his gear. After an uneventful fatigue detail, he walked over to the 6th with friends from his regiment to visit Thomas Hawkins and Alexander Kelly.

The general air of malaise in the camp mirrored the greater malaise of the nation. In Washington, D.C., thousands gathered on New Year's Day to watch the statue of the heroic, helmeted woman depicting Freedom raised to the top of the Capitol building. The statue had lain for months across the congressional lawn, its legs grotesquely sticking skyward as if the figure had been depicted in midfall. It seemed a fitting, unfortunate symbol of the direction of the country.

Some wondered, not too softly, if construction of the Capitol building and the ornate statue of the gallant lady were extravagances the nation could afford. The United States, after all, had suffered many deprivations and losses as a result of the ongoing catastrophic civil war. But Lincoln disagreed. "If people see the Capitol going on, it is a sign we intend the Union shall go on," he reasoned.

The statue was set upright and lifted to the top of the Capitol at noon—a symbol, Lincoln prayed, that the country would soon be set aright as well.

As 1864 opened, Lincoln was more determined than ever to bring the war to an end. One of the president's greatest fears was leaving the White House with a country still divided. The coming election in November made progress on the battlefield crucial. If the war didn't appear to be coming to a close by November, Lincoln's reelection hopes were bleak.

But as the New Year dawned, there was little hope for the prompt resolution of fighting. Lincoln had concluded that General George A. Meade was not the man to lead his army. He summoned a meeting with the hero of Vicksburg and Chattanooga, General Ulysses S. Grant. Lincoln had never met Grant and only knew of him by reputation and report, but he had come to think of him as his best fighter. A friend of Grant's showed the president a personal letter from the general, in which he stated that Lincoln was the best man for the Oval Office. With Grant's allegiance and absence of political ambitions confirmed, the matter was settled for Lincoln.

At Lincoln's prompting, the U.S. Congress was moving to revive the rank of lieutenant general, last held by General

George Washington. This would be the first formal step toward giving Grant command of the entire Union army.

In the South, the affairs of state were even more desperate. The New Year found Confederate president Jefferson Davis scrambling to feed Lee's army in Virginia. The South's financial position had always been more precarious than the Union's. "I cannot see how the mere material obstacles are to be sur-mounted" in order to bring an end to hostilities, a clearly frus-trated Davis noted.

The war was at a virtual standstill in January, with fighting limited to small skirmishes. The bulk of both armies camped near their respective capitals, Meade near Washington and Lee in the wilderness outside of Richmond.

Despite the winter lull, the business of war continued. Recruiters for the 38th U.S. Colored Infantry were in Yorktown on the first day of 1864. They signed up Edward Ratcliff, a twenty-nine-year-old laborer from James County, Virginia, who, nine months later, would see brutal combat at New Market Heights.

There were other reminders that the war continued. News came that two hundred Union soldiers had been captured in Jonesville, Virginia. Union officials worried about their fate after Jefferson Davis promised to hang them.

For Fleetwood, the early weeks of January were a blur of monotony, loneliness, and efforts to stay warm. He also worried about his health after experiencing sudden bouts of diarrhea, a condition likely linked to the poor hygiene in the camp.

On most days, he followed the same routine with military regularity—fatigue duty, writing reports, and reading letters. The boredom was palpable and beginning to take its toll. With little to do besides paperwork and chores, he grew restless and homesick, and increasingly complained about the loneliness of camp life.

His fits of melancholy were not surprising. Fleetwood was accustomed to the social life in Baltimore, evenings of debates and conversation and music. The evenings in a military camp in winter were quite different. He and other soldiers would gather to talk about home, the war, and, of late, the oppressive cold. Most of all, they wondered how long they would have to wait to fight.

Fleetwood's education and wide interests won him many admirers among white officers and black soldiers alike. He had gained a solid reputation among his white superiors, who considered him among the best, if not the best, of the black non-commissioned officers. Highly educated, with a natural inclination toward military matters, he was far better qualified than many of the white commissioned officers who, because of their race, held superior positions. He often wrote letters for officers as well as some of the soldiers who couldn't write or struggled badly with that form of communication.

As Fleetwood and his fellow soldiers waited in the miserable cold for the call to action, he understood better than most that the longer the war dragged on the more desperate both sides would become. If his suspicions proved true, the days ahead would likely be fraught with far greater danger than anything he and his regiment had so far experienced.

With little happening in the war, he asked for a furlough but was denied. Bored and cold, he read everything he could get his hands on, eager for any news of the broader war. He was enthralled by a lengthy article in a borrowed copy of January's *Atlantic Monthly* that summed up the progress of the war in a positive light for the Union and the antislavery cause. The story mentioned Grant's Vicksburg victory, which it labeled an operation of "the highest order of military excellence, and justly entitle [Grant] to be called a great soldier."

Fleetwood was pleased to see the magazine opine that there was a growing sentiment throughout the country that this was no longer just a white man's war. The abolition of slavery in rebel states rejuvenated the war effort, the *Atlantic Monthly* argued. Not only did it keep England from recognizing the South, but it gave the North the moral justification for preserving the Union.

"The Proclamation, therefore, even if it could be proved that it had not led to the liberation of one slave, has been of immense service to us, and the President deserves the thanks of every loyal American for having issued it. He threw a shell into the foreign Secession camp, the explosion of which was fatal to that 'cordial understanding' that was to have operated for our annihilation. Such was the year of the Proclamation, and its history is marvellous in our eyes. It stands in striking contrast to the other years of the war, both of which closed badly for us, and left the impression that the enemy's case was a good one, speaking militarily. Our improved condition should be attributed to the true cause."

It was heartening news for Fleetwood, a reminder of why he sat in a frigid military camp in the heart of winter, and not in the warm, safe confines of his Baltimore home.

The presence of a growing number of Federal troops at Yorktown, within striking distance of the Confederate capital of Richmond, didn't go unnoticed. Rebel scouts were watching closely. Robert E. Lee himself mentioned the concentration of troops in a dispatch a few days later. He doubted that they planned an attack, but sought to know what they were doing. He fully intended to watch them closely.

Others were also uneasy with the presence of the troops.

The black soldiers received an especially cold reception from the Virginia communities they guarded. Instead of hailing them as protectors of the region, residents acted with alarm at the sight of armed black soldiers roaming the countryside.

Virginia governor Francis. H. Pierpont, appointed by Lincoln over parts of the state under Union control, wrote a strong letter to Secretary of War Stanton on January 27, expressing his grave concerns over the deployment of black troops in his state. Despite the reputation for discipline and commitment to following orders for which the black troops had become known during their early tenure of service, they were never far removed from the reach of prejudice.

Governor Pierpont felt black troops should not be assigned roving patrol duties, since discipline in even veteran white regiments broke down when men were out of sight of their commanders. "These colored troops are new recruits just from bondage," he said. "Their own welfare requires discipline, hence their place in the field or fortification where they can be under the eye of their officers." He suggested that the black troops might be better served by an assignment to the front lines, otherwise "evil-disposed persons will circulate the news through the army that colored troops are sent back for guard duty, where there is no danger, while the white man is sent into the front of the battle."

White women and children feared for their safety around armed black men, Pierpont insisted. "But the great objection is the positive insolence of these colored soldiers, undisciplined as they are, to the white citizen. It is at the risk of the life of the citizen that we make any complaint of their bad conduct. I know you would not leave your wife and daughters in a community of armed Negroes, undisciplined and just liberated from bondage, with no other armed protection."

By even the most generous reading, Pierpont's letter was virulently racist. Now he labored to soften his bigotry. He pointed out that Virginia was doing more than its part for the Union cause, even to the extent of a new state constitution that would likely abolish slavery. Under the new constitution, slave owners in Virginia stood to lose six to eight thousand slaves, a painful loss, he said, that they were being forced to bear. He apologized to Stanton for troubling him with these complaints but said he felt duty bound to do so.

Fleetwood and other troops would have welcomed a transfer to the front. But in January, no clear front existed. The country and soldiers on both sides were frustrated by the inertia of the commanders. Fleetwood's terse January 25 diary entry summed up his dissatisfaction: "Nothing to do in camp."

But Union leaders were far from idle. In the frigid days of January, they were hatching a plan for a daring prison rescue in the very heart of the Confederate power. The plan called for black troops to play a critical role. General Butler planned to launch a series of attacks on Richmond to free prisoners being held at the infamous Libby Prison, a giant converted warehouse near the waterfront that housed mainly captive Union officers.

The Confederate capital lay about sixty miles from the Federal line around the Williamsburg peninsula. Lee could quickly send reinforcements. But his main focus was Meade's army in northern Virginia. The only troops permanently stationed around the heart of the South were detached soldiers and convalescents. The fortifications around the city consisted of strong stone batteries. But these were thinly manned and vulnerable to surprise. Union commanders felt the city was not well protected and could be entered on a swift strike.

General Wistar was given command of six thousand men, including the 4th, 5th, and 6th Colored regiments under

Colonel Samuel A. Duncan, for the raid. Wistar believed the success of the attack rested on surprising the enemy with a quick cavalry strike under the cover of darkness at the battery outside the city. "Without [a surprise], it would be impossible for cavalry alone to pass Battery No. 2," he wrote.

The large assembly of troops arriving at Fort Magruder raised eyebrows and sent rumors flying about a possible attack. The news didn't escape a Union private named William Boyle of the New York Mounted Rifles, waiting to be hanged for the murder of a lieutenant. His execution had been delayed by President Lincoln, who had suspended all executions for capital crimes to ease some of the tension of the war. On February 2, Boyle convinced the sentinel guarding him to help him escape. He slipped out of Fort Magruder and ultimately ended up in Richmond. He told rebel officials that a large number of cavalry and infantry units had been arriving at the fort and an attack on Richmond was imminent. The sentinel who helped him escape was later tried, convicted, and shot.

But Union officials, unaware of the treachery of Boyle, continued their planned attack. Excitement spread throughout the camp when the order to pull out came on February 5. This was what the men had waited for.

This was to be a lightning strike on an unsuspecting enemy. The men were told to pack six days' rations and thirty rounds of ammunition. Another forty rounds of ammunition for each soldier would be carried on the wagons. As men gathered up their tents and gear, Fleetwood took a moment to write brief letters to his mother and a friend.

At about 2 P.M. on February 5, Veal, Hilton, and Fleetwood lined up with the rest of the 4th for the march to Fort Magruder to join the other units. Beaty, Bronson, Holland, and Pinn were with the 5th, Hawkins and Kelly with the 6th. The drums signaled the beginning of the march as the colors flapped in a brisk, strong wind. The men began to sing and soon the regiments sounded like choir of deep, resounding voices.

The troops made good time. But the march was rough on Fleetwood, whose ill-fitting new shoes left his feet painfully sore and blistered. The soldiers arrived near Williamsburg at Fort Magruder shortly after nightfall the same day. A total of four thousand foot soldiers were there, accompanied by another twenty-two hundred cavalry riders. Along with Duncan's three black regiments were three white regiments that included Colonel R. M. West's 1st Pennsylvania and some light artillery units. It was an impressive array of military might.

The soldiers set up camp in the frigid February air. Fleetwood found a spot next to a bush. He felt somewhat disoriented in the unfamiliar landscape and sudden clutter of activity. That night he had a strange dream that he was in China.

The twenty-two hundred cavalry riders moved out on the morning of February 6, two hours before the infantry. The five mounted regiments were under Colonel S. P. Spear, 11th Pennsylvania Cavalry. Wistar ordered the riders to arrive at Bottom's Bridge, twelve miles directly east of Richmond and six miles from Libby Prison, by 3 A.M. the next day.

Bottom's Bridge spanned the Chickahominy River where the road from Williamsburg to Richmond meets the river. Near it was a Confederate fortification called Battery No. 2. The plan was for the cavalry to surprise and capture the sleeping Confederate soldiers and silence their guns before rushing ahead to spring open the doors to Richmond and Libby Prison.

The element of surprise was paramount. Wistar mapped out a roundabout route to avoid detection by rebel scouts—a fifty-one-mile journey, much of it in darkness. The cavalry's mission was to break through the fortifications at Battery No. 2 and then ride rapidly to Richmond. If successful, they would occupy Capitol Square in the city for two or three hours to release prisoners before Lee could reinforce the city. If possible, the cavalry was to try to capture Confederate president Jefferson Davis, which would likely end the war.

Wistar's orders even listed Davis's home address: "Major Wheelan, with 300 of First New York Mounted Rifles, will turn to the right and capture Jeff. Davis at his residence, corner Twelfth and Marshall streets." General Butler had inside information about Jefferson Davis's residence and habits: one of the guides along for the mission was a former gardener of the Confederate president who had since deserted to the loyalists.

"If we could have laid our hands upon Davis in the early morning he would certainly have taken a ride to Fortress Monroe to greet an old friend of his who would have taken special care to keep him there, certainly as long as the telegraph wires would not work between there and Washington so that the President's pardon could not reach him," Butler later wrote.

Davis's "former friend" was none other than the cockeyed Butler himself, who in 1860 voted fifty-seven times on successive ballots to make Davis the Democratic candidate for president of the United States. At the time, Davis was still loyal and served as secretary of war under President Pierce.

Other Union riders were ordered to target Belle Island, freeing prisoners there and destroying public buildings, factories, storehouses, and the Tredegar Iron Works, a sprawling five-acre manufacturing site that produced ammunition and artillery critical to the Confederate army. The Union prisoners at Libby would then be taken back across Bottom's Bridge under the protection of the black regiments.

To make sure that Confederate scouts and guards couldn't warn the rebel battery of the cavalry's advance, a handpicked company was placed under Captain Hill of the 1st New York Mounted Rifles, with the best horses selected. They were to gallop ahead of the cavalry and ride down the rebel guards at New Kent, Baltimore Cross-Roads, and at the bridge. If the guards could be captured, the Union soldiers could surprise and overrun the entrenchment. Arrangements were made to cut the telegraph wires between Meadow Station and Richmond between dark and midnight that night.

In the early morning hours of February 6, Fleetwood followed the movements of the horses and riders as the cavalry moved out. Then his eyes returned to his morning report, which he completed with some difficulty in the numbing cold. Fortunately, his feet felt better. He had gladly traded his new shoes with a drummer for an old beat-up, worn pair.

The orders to move out and advance toward Richmond came a few hours later. The men cheered loudly; the battle was at hand. They began the thirty-three-mile journey to New Kent Court House, where Wistar planned to set up his headquarters. The march took them through Williamsburg by 10 A.M., two miles from Fort Magruder. From there, they marched northwest along the forest-lined Williamsburg Road between the York and Chickahominy rivers toward the Confederate capital.

"We hoped to be inside the fortifications of Richmond before 9 o'clock A.M., of February 7th," said one soldier in the regiment with Hawkins and Kelly. "Beyond that we made little calculation further than to do our best." They marched throughout the day in the frosty February temperatures to the percussive beat of the drummers, unaware that the enemy was watching their every move.

Rebel scouts, hidden in the woods, crept up to the advancing line of black troops, just a few feet away at times. Confederate major Eppa Hunton's report the next morning was ample proof of this. "One of my men . . . has just arrived to give the particulars of the late advance of the enemy. He says he was in 15 yards of the column when it passed. It consisted of one brigade of cavalry, three brigades of infantry, and twelve pieces of artillery. He says that independent of this force there was a large force below, 3 miles below the Burnt Ordinary. He could form no accurate idea of this force, as they were below the scouts; judged it was large from the incessant beating of drums."

So much for the element of surprise. The Union attack quickly encountered other problems. The cavalry failed to round up the Confederate advance guards in the area. It was becoming obvious to Union soldiers that the rebels knew they were coming. "We felt sure before midnight of the first days' march that our coming was known, for two or three times we saw sky rockets go up some distance in advance of us, no doubt signals of approaching danger," Captain John McMurray noted.

Union officers confirmed their worst fears when captured Confederate prisoners affirmed the planned attack was no secret. Prisoners questioned personally by Wistar concurred in saying that the escaped murderer Boyle was captured in the area after a chase that left him exhausted. He had unveiled the Union plan to capture Richmond, and was immediately sent on a relay of horses to the capital.

Wistar was furious. He pointed out that Boyle would have been hanged long ago if not for Lincoln's order. With their plans becoming more untenable by the minute, Union officers decided to press on with the raid.

The black infantry marched on through a long, tiring advance in the cold night with no opposition. They stopped at Burnt Ordinary for a short rest and then moved on until dinner at 1 A.M., stopping just long enough to eat. The regiment then headed to New Kent Court House, arriving by 2:30 A.M. The frigid, wet weather and pressing pace proved devastating. The march left the men "completely broken down," Fleetwood noted.

Meanwhile, the cavalry neared their objective at Bottom's Bridge, about seven miles away, at 2:50 A.M., ten minutes ahead of schedule. They readied for their surprise charge.

But the enemy had been waiting for hours. The Confederates had assembled a strong force that included four batteries of artillery and three regiments of infantry as well as cavalry. More troops were arriving on the York River Railroad. The cavalry found that the bridge planks had been taken up and all the fords across the river were obstructed. The rebels had dug hundreds of rifle pits, and extensive earthworks were constructed along the river.

The rebels had been preparing for the battle for sixteen hours, according to local residents who were interviewed by Union officers. The black residents who welcomed them told the same story. News of their arrival might as well have been announced in the newspapers.

To add to the Union obstacles, the weather was turning hazy and wet. The unusually dark night made an attack impossible until daylight. As dawn broke, Major James Wheelan decided to carry out the cavalry's mission despite the obvious problems. His regiment, along with Lieutenant Colonel Benjamin F. Onderdonk's riders, found an approachable ford across the Chickahominy and readied to charge. The road the cavalry took to the creek was worn to a depth of several feet in the soft soil by heavy use, and the rut in the track was narrow, forcing the horsemen to ride in twos. As they turned to enter the bridge, they saw that the planks had been removed. The Union and enemy advance guards exchanged fire.

Prisoners captured earlier by Union forces reported that the Confederate batteries were no longer thinly manned, but were now occupied by a large force of soldiers. The men in the front of the column noticed two heavy guns aimed in their direction. Before they could react, the guns belched and three horsemen fell.

The cavalry sprang toward the ford. The soldiers yelled loudly as the horses lunged forward in a furious gallop, sending up cascading water all around them. The rebels, comfortably entrenched on the other side, opened fire on the narrow ford in the river. Men and horses went down in the water and along the shore. Cavalrymen continued to charge, but were repulsed by the fire from the battery. Nine men were killed or wounded and ten horses lost.

The riders took the dead and wounded from the field, along with their saddles and equipment. Scouts were sent up and down the river for several miles looking for any possible crossing. But at each ford, the enemy was found in force with newly placed obstacles. The attack had been anything but a surprise.

At least three regiments of rebel infantry were identified as having fired from the woods. But it was anyone's guess how many were hidden in the brush. Four batteries of field artillery were counted. The rebels had even brought out a heavy gun, which could certainly reach Union forces where they were gathered. The first few shots landed to the rear of Union troops.

The problems for the Union forces kept compounding. When rebel commander Hunton passed on an update of initial skirmishes with Union forces to his commanders in Richmond, he wasn't breaking any news. They already knew. The Federal efforts to destroy the Confederate telegraph wires had failed.

Unaware that the initial Union attack had faltered, Hilton, Veal, Fleetwood, and their regiments pulled out at 6 A.M. on February 7 to meet up with the cavalry near Bottom's Bridge. They arrived at about noon.

But by then, Wistar had decided to withdraw his troops. The possibility of a surprise attack had vanished. Proceeding against an entrenched enemy would mean a heavy loss of life, and there was no way to reach Richmond now. "There remained no object to be gained commensurate with the loss and jeopardy to be incurred by delay," Wistar wrote, "and my orders were explicit—that if the surprise failed, the command was not to be risked for any new object."

The black infantry regiments were within seven miles of the bridge when they met the head of the returning cavalry column. Wistar decided to retire the whole force. The black regiments stood aside while the cavalry passed, and three hundred men from the 3rd New York Cavalry were retained as the rear guard.

The men noted the dejection and disappointment on the faces of the cavalry riders. Their dreams of galloping through Richmond under the morning sun had given way to embarrassment and defeat. The men wondered aloud if they would ever get to Richmond now.

Rebel soldiers launched a pursuit. They attacked at Baltimore Store, where the 3rd New York Cavalry drove them back with the help from a nearby Union battery. The rebel commanders were confused by the Union retreat. Confederate major Hunton thought it must be a trick. "A dispatch just received from Colonel Shingler says his cavalry pursued the enemy to Crump's Cross-Roads, which is about 5 miles. Now, if this report of the forces of the enemy is correct (and I have no doubt of it), I am at a loss to understand why the enemy has retired for the small repulse received. Query: Have they abandoned the object of the expedition? I do not yet feel sure of it."

He wondered if they were searching for another avenue toward the city. "They brought very few wagons (not over fifteen or twenty in all), and a rapid raid only seems to have been contemplated. It would not surprise me if they had fallen back to make a better start, probably on some other road. I shall keep up the utmost diligence until I am satisfied."

But no such raid was being contemplated.

The infantry marched back to New Kent Court House two days after the expedition began and tented down for the night. Disappointment over the failure of the mission and the frustration of not coming head to head with the rebels hit Fleetwood. His regiment had marched 104 miles with the rest of the infantry without being able offer anything more than light fire in return. Fleetwood was "intensely disgusted." The infantry soldiers couldn't help but wonder what would have happened had they been able to cross at Bottom's Bridge. The marching and camp life was beginning to wear on him. He longed for the decisive battle that would settle the war in the Union's favor. Sadly, the aborted raid on Richmond was not that battle.

Wistar wrote to Butler, expressing his dissatisfaction over the mission. "I regret your disappointment. It is no greater, I assure you, than mine. More might have been done . . . attacking the bridge; but under the circumstances, distance from base, no available troops in department to reinforce me, evident preparation by enemy, and, above all, the entire defeat of the real object—in any event it would not have been wise in my judgment. Was I right?"

The next day, the black regiments marched under the watch of the rebel scouts, who tallied their numbers and reported back to Hunton. Fleetwood, who was beginning to feel ill, was with the regiments when they halted for lunch at Williamsburg. They marched through the city that had once been the nation's capital, where George Washington fell in love with Martha Custis, who became his wife. Williamsburg had fallen on hard times and had become a tumbledown town of a couple hundred poor whites and blacks. About half a mile long with one main street of thirty homes, it was now the center of an active oyster trade.

Every time the regiments marched through Williamsburg, the main street was lined by black residents waving and cheering encouragement. They were proud of their soldiers. The excitement was contagious. At the end of the street a black woman danced to the point of near exhaustion at seeing troops of her color. Some of the men noticed a group of black residents on a portico. Among them was a beautiful young woman watching the soldiers. She laughed and talked as they went by. A handsome soldier from the 6th Regiment, Nathaniel Danks, broke ranks and sprang up the steps of the portico to kiss her on the cheek with an exaggerated smack. Then he dashed away before she could properly react. A cheer went up from the men. Danks was the hero of the day.

It was moments like this that reminded Fleetwood of what he was truly fighting for. He was deeply moved by the pride displayed by blacks in the city as they marched by. These were the people he was prepared to die for, and their wild cheers made him walk a just little taller.

When the men returned to camp, letters from six friends were waiting for Fleetwood. He settled down to read news from home, so distant from the war. Later, he washed up and retired to a welcome sleep.

Wistar wrote out reports of the mission, again praising the black infantry units. He noted that they had marched in four days "33, 28, 18, and 25 miles, respectively, with alacrity and cheerfulness, and almost without straggling, the colored troops being in this respect, as usual, remarkable."

Butler may have been disappointed in the mission, but he was satisfied with Wistar's handling of the affair: "The operation was skillfully and brilliantly done. It gives the commanding general renewed confidence in General Wistar as a commander of a division."

Butler wrote Secretary of War Stanton informing him that the mission was thwarted by a murderous Union soldier awaiting death who had escaped and revealed plans of the attack to the enemy. The man's hanging had been delayed by Lincoln's orders suspending executions. Here, Butler, who had ambitions on the presidency himself, gently laid some of the blame on the president and asked that he revoke his policy.

The attack on Richmond failed, Butler believed, "only from one of those fortuitous circumstances against which no foresight can provide and no execution can overcome. By the corruption and faithlessness of a sentinel, who is now being tried for the offense, a man condemned to death, but reprieved by the President, was allowed to escape within the enemy's lines, and there gave them such information as enabled them to meet our advance."

He found ample evidence that the convicted Union soldier was to blame in the Richmond papers, the *Examiner* and the *Sentinel*, which published articles the day after the attack confirming Boyle's role. A flag-of-truce boat from Richmond brought a copy of the *Examiner*, whose story read, "Some days since a report was obtained by the authorities here from a Yankee deserter that the enemy was contemplating a raid in considerable force on Richmond." The article's claims were consistent with the statements of captured rebels.

Butler also agreed with Wistar that the raid had not been in vain. Fears in Richmond over an attack would likely divert troops from other battlefronts. "I beg leave to call your attention to the suggestion of General Wistar in his report that the effect of the raid will be to hereafter keep as many troops around

Richmond for its defense from any future movement of the Army of the Potomac as we have in this neighborhood."

Wistar was correct in this regard. Confederate president Davis told General Lee that the Union army had descended "in force" to Bottom's Bridge. Lee sent General Pickett, who was returning from an unsuccessful foray to New Bern, North Carolina, to Richmond.

The reward for the black infantry units after four days of marching was a day off. Fleetwood spent the vacation resting and reading the first volume of *Les Misérables*. He played dominoes, sang, and "lazied" about, waiting for the inevitable call to action. His thoughts turned, as they often did, to home and the very different life he had left behind.

—∞∞∞—

SEVEN

AVENGING AN AMBUSH

By February 11, Fleetwood's regiment was back into its normal routine. He made out reports and performed guard duty. The newspapers carried a report that six horses in the White House stables had died during a fire. President Lincoln had tried to get the animals out but failed.

Fleetwood wrote letters in the afternoon, followed by a battalion drill. In the evening, the regiment was out of water. He spent the time reading the second volume of *Les Misérables* and fell asleep thirsty.

While black regiments in Virginia waited impatiently to see action, events unfolding hundreds of miles away would seriously impact how military officials viewed them as a fighting force. Federal forces had arrived in Jacksonville, Florida, on February 7 to disrupt the movement of supplies to Confederate units in the state, recruit blacks, and help establish a pro-Union state government. In the first two weeks, they encountered little opposition, but on February 20, Brigadier General Truman Seymour and fifty-five hundred Federal troops—including black soldiers—

marched to meet Confederate forces camped near Olustee. The forces met in the open, fighting without earthworks or fortifications. In the ensuing bloodfest, two of the Union regiments gave way in the confusion of the battle, leaving the 8th U.S. Colored Troops to bear the brunt of the enemy's attack.

The black regiment, whose ranks were filled with raw recruits with just two months' training, was on the left of the Union line. They had advanced to about a thousand yards of the enemy line when their commanding officer, Colonel Charles Fribley, got the order to put them into the fray. They faced the entire left wing of the rebel army, which opened a heavy fire from close range on the unprotected soldiers. Colonel Fribley was killed. Major Loren Burritt took over and then was hit twice. The regiment held its ground for some time. Three color sergeants and five of the color guard were killed. The regiment was driven back after five ferocious hours of fighting, leaving its colors and the Confederates in command of the battlefield. More than three hundred soldiers from the regiment were killed, including thirty of the forty-three in the color guard company.

Total battle casualties amounted to 1,861 Union and 946 Confederate soldiers. In proportion to the number of troops involved, it was one of the bloodiest battles of the Civil War.

News of the fall of the black regiment was painful among black soldiers, especially those in Gardner and James's 36th Regiment. The men knew some of the officers; one had been with the 36th before going to Florida. "I hope that no stigma will be attached to our regiment for what was, I believe, the unavoidable loss of our colors," wrote R. C. Bailey, a captain of the 8th U.S. Colored Troops.

The doubts raised about the fighting abilities of blacks were the same that dogged them from the start. When white troops suffered defeats, their losses were discussed in terms of poor military tactics and insufficient numbers of troops. But for blacks, Fleetwood and others noted wryly, each defeat was directly attributable to race. It was a lesson the black troops took to heart, always conscious that they represented an entire race each time they stepped onto the battlefield.

Even as questions resurfaced about the suitability of black soldiers for combat, Union officials were again contemplating using them in a renewed effort to free prisoners held in Richmond. On Sunday, February 28, a large cavalry expedition headed out from Williamsburg under the command of Brigadier General Judson Kilpatrick with thirty-five hundred men. The black regiments were ordered to prepare for a march. Fleetwood spent the day packing, reading, and resting for the journey.

Nicknamed "Kill Cavalry" by his men, Kilpatrick was just twenty-eight, an unpredictable commander with strong political connections. He was a tightly wound, "wiry, restless, undersized man with black eyes, a lantern jaw," who was considered young for a brigadier general. A member of Meade's staff once said it was hard to look at Kilpatrick without laughing.

Kilpatrick graduated from the U.S. Military Academy in 1861. He entered the war a second lieutenant in May and was wounded at Big Bethel in June. Promoted to lieutenant colonel in September of that year, he commanded a regiment defending Washington. He had also fought in a previous raid on Richmond and at the battle of Gettysburg.

Kilpatrick's plans to raid Richmond were part of a grand design hatched in Washington with the blessings and encouragement of President Lincoln, who was anxious for another strike at the enemy. Richmond's prisons were crowded and Union officials were anxious to free soldiers held there. Kilpatrick had convinced the president and Stanton to allow him to seize the city and distribute amnesty proclamations within enemy lines.

Given the go-ahead, Kilpatrick crossed the Rapidan on Sunday, February 28, with 2,375 men. Among his commanders was George Armstrong Custer, who had distinguished himself at Gettysburg by protecting the Union flank on the last day of battle. The riders rode out in the darkness under splendid weather that seemed like a gift from above.

Kilpatrick split his army, sending Colonel Ulric Dahlgren and five hundred cavalry riders to Goochland, about thirty miles north of Richmond. They were ordered to cross the James River and attack Richmond at the same time Kilpatrick's forces struck from the north. Dahlgren was just twenty-two, but had already distinguished himself in the war. He was the son of the venerated admiral John Dahlgren, the inventor of the Dahlgren gun, the massive, soda-bottle-shaped canon that devastated ships and battlements alike.

The younger Dahlgren studied civil engineering and law before becoming Major General Franz Sigel's aide. He was promoted to Sigel's chief of artillery at the Second Bull Run. He later served as General Ambrose Burnside's aide. At Chancellorsville he was on General Joseph Hooker's staff, and at Gettysburg on Meade's. On the retreat from Gettysburg, he was severely wounded in the foot and his leg was amputated. He was promoted to colonel and returned to duty on crutches. A superior praised the well-connected Dahlgren to Kilpatrick as a man of "gallantry, intelligence, and energy."

Kilpatrick's men met with some resistance at Ely's Ford, where they captured fifteen Confederates, and at Beaver Dam Station near Taylorsville, where Union men destroyed the railroad depot, water tanks, a storehouse, and pulled up and burned track. They cut telegraph wire and poles. They even tried to capture a railroad train, but the conductor spotted the burning buildings ahead and returned to Richmond.

For Fleetwood and soldiers in his fellow black regiments theirs was now a waiting game. The men talked about the news that troops were heading toward Richmond and wondered if they would get a chance to attack the city. They didn't have to wonder long. Marching orders came the next day.

Butler ordered the black regiments under Colonel Duncan through Williamsburg to the New Kent Court House to stand ready if Richmond should fall. The men formed a line in the pouring rain and began the journey. They marched under heavy showers for more than twenty miles along mud-soaked roads, impassable except by foot. It was slow, slogging going. Fleetwood, however, was spared the march because of a bout of sickness that confined him to bed. He slept in a featherbed on March 1, a rare treat.

For the other soldiers, it was a wretched march. "It was very dark and the roads were in miserable condition," wrote a white lieutenant in the same regiment as Beaty, Bronson, and Holland. "One of the worst nights I ever experienced. We passed through Williamsburg shortly after dark. The citizens kept well within doors. Afraid of the 'nigger' I suppose."

The next day, the black regiments marched to New Kent Court House, within twenty miles of Richmond. "Forty-four miles in twenty three hours!" the same lieutenant wrote. "Whew! How my legs ache."

Word came that Sedgwick and Custer succeeded in reaching their destinations and were able to cut off the city before the rebels could detect an attack on the capital. Kilpatrick had little difficulty reaching Richmond on Tuesday, March 1. His advance wasn't even noticed until he was near the city.

But the general quickly found that he had underestimated

the strength of the city's defenses. Once again, rebel scouts sounded the alarm and Lee was able to rush defenses to the city. Dahlgren's army was nowhere in sight and not returning signals in the cloud-filled, misty sky. Kilpatrick's army was pushed back by infantry and artillery fire, making a successful attack highly improbable. After some quick skirmishing, the general decided to withdraw to Williamsburg and return with the black troops and Butler's army.

Unaware of Kilpatrick's decision, the black troops were on their way to the Confederate capital. They could hear the sound of cannons echoing in the distance and wondered if Kilpatrick was upon the city. Then a courier came bounding down the road on horseback. He brought the news that the infantry need not advance further, and that Kilpatrick was retreating. The sounds of heavy guns were Union forces firing at Southern guerrillas.

The black soldiers halted to rest their aching legs. Kilpatrick's men soon appeared, somewhat exhilarated over their close encounter with Richmond. The black troops waited as six thousand cavalry and twelve pieces of artillery slowly worked their way down the muddy Virginia road. "The boys told us that they had been within two miles of Richmond and had thrown shot and shell in that direction for an hour," Lieutenant James J. Scroggs, a white officer in the 5th U.S. Colored Infantry, stated wistfully.

Colonel Dahlgren had failed to reach the city on schedule to launch a simultaneous attack with Kilpatrick. He had been misled by a black slave boy by the name of Martin, whom he had secured as a guide. The slave had said he could take the men to a ford in the James River. But instead the guide became lost and brought them to a high bank without a ford. Dahlgren ordered him hanged from a tree.

Dahlgren's men pushed down the left bank of the river and came near Richmond just as Kilpatrick was withdrawing. He tried to advance, but the cover of night prevented him. He decided to withdraw and join the main body of Kilpatrick's army.

The next day Dahlgren's men moved out to find Kilpatrick's force already headed back to Williamsburg. They rode quietly through King William County, where locals reported their presence to the Confederates' 9th Virginia Cavalry. The rebels pursued and fired at his party from the rear near Bruington Church, and a fight that lasted for several miles ensued. For the time being, Dahlgren and his troops escaped unharmed and halted and fed near Mantapike, where they commandeered grain and supplies from the locals.

The rebel sniping at his rear was merely a ploy to slow him down. The Confederates had collected a handpicked group of men from different commands to drive ahead and wait in ambush in the woods. The rebel shooters settled under the brush and waited for the cavalry to march through.

After an hour or two of rest, Ulric Dahlgren's men moved out, the colonel himself and about fifty men riding in the advance guard ahead of main body of their force. Dahlgren's group entered the woods and traveled along a winding trail. The rebels waited patiently, holding their fire until the head of the Union column was within a few yards. Then they let loose with full fury. Colonel Dahlgren was hit, and then again. He was hit even as he fell. Five balls ripped through his body. He lay mortally wounded as the rest of his men frantically tried to escape the trap. But they were helpless as the Confederates opened volley after volley into the confused Union ranks. The rebels, with just 150 men, surrounded the cavalry and captured 175 prisoners, including 38 blacks, several horses, and weapons.

Dahlgren's body was stripped by rebels and tossed on a road, where some Union sympathizers found it naked and badly mutilated. The rebels recovered a package of papers and orders from Dahlgren that would add a bit of mystery to the mission.

Dahlgren's death sent shock waves throughout the chain of command, up to the desk of President Lincoln. Dahlgren's father was one of the most illustrious, decorated commanders in the U.S. Navy. He heard reports that his son may have been killed or captured and sent a message to President Lincoln asking for any information. But no word of his son's fate had yet reached Washington.

Butler initially was informed that the colonel had been captured. A deserter reported that a one-legged colonel was among the prisoners taken in the area. Then came word of his death and that his naked corpse had been left on public display on a road.

Lincoln telegraphed Butler urgently asking about Dahlgren's body. General Butler was told that Union friends had taken it into hiding and wrote Admiral Dahlgren with the information. Confirmation of Dahlgren's fate came from Confederate newspapers.

General Meade read a report in the *Richmond Sentinel* that Dahlgren was killed. "I fear the account is true," he telegraphed Major General Henry Wager Halleck. "The paper will be sent you to-morrow."

The ordeal had charged passions on both sides. To add to the drama, Richmond newspapers carried a story of a secret mission assigned to Dahlgren. Papers taken from his body were allegedly orders to burn Richmond and kill President Davis, his cabinet, and General Lee. The text of the address was printed in the *Richmond Daily Examiner*, which called it a "diabolical design." The headline read: FULL DISCLOSURE OF THE ENEMY'S

PLANS—RICHMOND TO BE DESTROYED—THE PRESIDENT AND HIS CABINET TO BE KILLED, ETC.

The article quoted Dahlgren's papers as stating, "You have been selected from brigades and regiments as a picked command to attempt a desperate undertaking, an undertaking which, if successful, will write your names on the hearts of your countrymen in letters that can never be erased, and which will cause the prayers of our fellow-soldiers now confined in loathsome prisons to follow you and yours wherever you may go. We hope to release the prisoners from Belle Island first, and having seen them fairly started, we will cross the James River into Richmond, destroying the bridges after us and exhorting the released prisoners to destroy and burn the hateful city; and do not allow the rebel leader Davis and his traitorous crew to escape."

While the article fueled Southern anger, Dahlgren's brutal death prompted calls for revenge from Union officials, among them Butler. He decided to send his black regiments with Kilpatrick "to deal with those citizens who, claiming to be noncombatants when any force of ours is there, yet turned out and ambushed Dahlgren." General Isaac Wistar, who had led the troops in October and February, was put in charge of the mission. Under his command were artillery and the black infantry regiments—about twenty-seven hundred men in all—including the 4th, 5th, 6th, and 22nd Colored Infantry.

The six-day expedition into enemy territory was a limited military success, with black troops again forced to suffer through a grueling advance in wet, cold, miserable weather. Kilpatrick, who led a cavalry regiment during the expedition, provided the following assessment of the effort in a letter to Butler: "The people about King and Queen Court-House have been well punished for the murder of Colonel Dahlgren. Colonel Onderdonk reports that the Fifth and Ninth Virginia Cavalry, with citizens—about 1,200 in all—were driven from their camp near Carlton's Store, the camp burned, several killed and wounded, and some 20 taken prisoners. The enemy was also driven from the Court-House, a large amount of rebel property destroyed, a mill filled with grain belonging to the Ninth Virginia Cavalry, and other buildings containing grain burned. General Wistar will return on Sunday."

During the military mission, the black troops had marched through a severe rainstorm under the strain of heavy gear. Lieutenant Scroggs was glowing in his praise: "Our men, laden down with their heavy knapsacks, shelter tents, four days' rations and eighty rounds of cartridges, were hurried along through the mud and rain, until they could bear their heavy loads no longer, and then they threw away their knapsacks containing their clothing and blankets, and marched steadily along. Yes, these men, these most faithful of all soldiers, who are now fighting for the salvation of a country to which they owe nothing but curses, for the miserable pittance of seven dollars per month; throw away their clothing which is an individual loss to each one, that they might be able to carry their gun and ammunition, and pursue the enemy swiftly."

The soldiers enjoyed some time off after the expedition. Fleetwood returned to his clerking duties the following day. He didn't attend guard mount or inspection but made the dress parade. He tried catching up on his letter writing in the evening but fell asleep after writing only a few. The following day was just as leisurely. Fleetwood spent it writing, except for taking time for the dress parade. Over the next two days, he visited with Hawkins, went horseback riding, and had a rare treat of peaches and milk.

But always, there was the war. Talk around the regiment was that another attack on Richmond was imminent. Union scouts also believed that the rebels were not sitting back waiting for an attack, but were just weeks away from launching their own offensive strike.

H. Lohman, an informant who claimed to be sent by Union sympathizers in Richmond, reported, "The enemy are making large preparations for the capture of Norfolk. Heavy details are made from Pickett's division to work on the gun-boats now building at Richmond. The work is pushed night and day, and it is expected three gun-boats will be finished in three or four weeks. They are also building floats or rafts to carry guns to move down the James River with their fleet. Longstreet is to have command on the Black water for the main attack on Norfolk. His whole command is expected at Petersburg. His force estimated at 15,000. Pontoons have been sent from Richmond to Petersburg. A feint will be made on Williamsburg with a force of 3,000 infantry, with some cavalry and artillery, and for this purpose Ford's Bridge over the Chickahominy is being rebuilt."

There was also a report that Confederate major general J. E. B. "Jeb" Stuart was collecting a cavalry force at Fredericksburg to make a raid on the Union rear. Stuart was apparently waiting for the Rappahannock to become fordable to cross around Fredericksburg. A great deal of supplies and ammunition had been sent over both roads that met at Hanover Junction.

So six days after returning from their mission to avenge Dahlgren's death, the black regiments were on the move again. This time, they were returning to familiar country.

On March 17, Butler ordered the black regiments back to Mathews County, an area they had explored the previous October on their first mission under General Wistar. As Fleetwood readied to leave, he jotted an excited note in his diary: "Preparing to leave for a raid."

He would have been even more excited had he known that even as the mission got under way, President Lincoln was urging leaders in Maryland to accept emancipation. The mood in Fleetwood's hometown was shifting toward the abolition of slavery. Leaders were drafting a new state constitution and Lincoln pressed for the document to abolish slavery.

Fleetwood lined up with Veal and Hilton and the rest of the 4th at noon. But the trip didn't get under way until after 5 P.M. The regiment loaded aboard a transport vessel at the Yorktown wharf.

General Charles Graham sent orders for the transport to follow his boat along the Piankatank River. The convoy included gunboats as well as the transports. Fleetwood found sailing downriver infinitely more pleasant than the grueling thirty-mile march of the previous expedition to Mathews County. The boats pushed along the river in the darkness since no one wanted to catch rebel fire from the water, and the convoy landed at midnight about eight miles from the Mathews County Court House, one of the key targets of the raid.

The black regiments disembarked and guards formed a defensive perimeter around the makeshift camp on the beach. Fleetwood was tired and tried to nap while waiting for orders. He was just falling asleep around 3:30 A.M. when the order came to move out.

The mission, as described by Colonel John W. Ames of the 6th U.S. Colored Troops, was for the soldiers to quickly occupy the county courthouse. They were to seize all suspicious characters, confiscate rebel property, and help blacks fleeing Southern tyranny. The soldiers were warned not to loot homes in the area.

The mission began with hiccups. No one in Fleetwood's regiment knew the way to the courthouse. Fleetwood and several other soldiers were sent house to house in search of a guide.

They marched off in the darkness into hostile territory and continued for some time without any luck until they came to a house set off by itself on a hill. It was obviously occupied and the soldiers broke in, surprising two rebel officers inside. One was captured, but the other escaped into the woods. The captured man was a cavalry officer, who, after repeated questioning, finally gave directions to the courthouse.

Even as the soldiers smiled at their good fortune, it was about to change. Rebels had crept close in the darkness and now had the house surrounded. They demanded the release of the prisoner, and, when their request was not complied with, opened fire. The black troops shot back. The gunfire attracted the larger Union force, and as more soldiers appeared the rebels beat a hasty retreat.

With directions in hand, the men began the eight-mile march to the courthouse. They traveled in the darkness and arrived by dawn. Just hours earlier, the building had been occupied by a rebel company, but now only a few stragglers were in the area. They were surprised by the sight of Union soldiers but managed to escape.

Colonel Ames moved to further secure the area. He wanted the men to march two miles to the Gloucester Road, where it ran by the East River. They were to create a three-mile line of sentinels from across the peninsula to an estuary of the Piankatank. The soldiers were ordered to pick up anybody who was acting as a rebel picket or scout and help blacks escaping the South get to waiting boats. The men were told to seize any property that might be useful.

The order was confusing to many soldiers, who failed to see the distinction between confiscating property and looting, against which they had been warned. Some saw it as a foraging mission.

Even Fleetwood showed some confusion. His diary entry that day, written in cryptic shorthand, reflected this: "Arrived at Matthews Coast. Houses took possession, and breakfasted. Went foraging. Loot house. Got horse harness and buggy."

The regimental line stretched for three miles, which left many of the men on their own and away from supervision or fellow soldiers. The line between confiscating useful property and pillaging quickly blurred and then vanished. Men broke into homes and pilfered jewelry and watches and personal items as well as food. Many of the residents abandoned their homes as the black troops approached. Soldiers ransacked homes, taking valuables from drawers and desks. "That the men began to consider the expedition a kind of plundering foray, rendered it almost impossible to execute this order while carrying out the letter of the others," noted Colonel George Rogers of the 4th U.S. Colored Troops. Residents were in an uproar.

In the afternoon, soldiers began returning with booty in hand. Colonel Rogers felt the mission was getting out of control. He ordered an inspection of the camp and collected everything the men had plundered from the residents. "The result was a motley collection of all kinds of fowl (dead and alive), fresh and cured meats, and a promiscuous heap of all of the smaller appliances of the culinary art, together with cloths, linens, ornaments of dress, and little objects," he reported.

Rogers was furious. He called for his officers and told them to use any means to stop the looting.

"What if they don't obey the order?" an officer asked.

"Shoot any enlisted man on the spot who continued to plunder," Rogers said.

The officers were sent out to gather the men. Lieutenant Charles Holcombe, Company E, caught a black soldier in the act of looting a home. He ordered the man to discard the items and leave the property. The soldier refused. Holcombe called for one his men and ordered him to shoot the looter. The order was promptly obeyed. The man was shot and lay writhing in pain on the floor, shot through but not mortally wounded.

Rogers, who was distressed that the raid had disintegrated into a plundering mission, felt the shooting "went a great way toward restoring the discipline of the regiment." Still, he worried that the looting incident could have a long-term effect on the psyche of the black troops. "I cannot close this report without the remark that whatever the object of the expedition, it was a misfortune that it produced a very demoralizing effect on this command. It is to be regretted that it is one of the effects of such an expedition to destroy in a week that discipline which it is the work of months to establish."

While the breakdown in discipline was an obvious concern, some saw the looting as a symptom of the larger problem of unequal pay between black and white soldiers in the military. Many of the black troops had entered the army as ex-slaves with no money to support or set up their families in the North. Unlike the families of white soldiers, the families of black troops received no financial support from the federal government. Many free blacks had left employment that paid much better than the army and had to obtain loans from friends for survival.

Black soldiers were still dealing with the backlash of the looting incident when the 38th Congress took up the equal pay debate in late March. On average, blacks made more than a third less than their white counterparts. Such unequal pay was obviously insulting and troubling for black soldiers, who faced the same risks in battle as whites. It also hindered their white commanders, who had to deal with the festering resentment the pay difference spawned among their black troops.

Lieutenant James J. Scroggs of the 5th U.S. Colored Infantry threatened to resign if Congress failed to equalize pay. In his diary, he wrote, "The rebels have not yet recognized or treated such colored soldiers as have fallen into their hands as prisoners of war, but have butchered, starved and even burnt them to death. Yet to these men, who voluntarily brave these dangers, our government pays but the poor pittance. Should this Congress adjourn without doing full and complete justice to the free colored volunteer it will deserve that 'perfidious' be attached to its number in history. I did not enter this service from any mercenary motive but to assist in removing the unreasonable prejudice against the colored race, and to contribute a share however small toward making the Negro an effective instrument in crushing out this unholy rebellion."

Calls from across the Union to correct the pay inequities took on a new sense of urgency after one of the most inhumane moments of the war. On April 12, a Confederate cavalry force led by former slave dealer Nathan Bedford Forrest—who would go on to be an early leader of the Ku Klux Klan—struck at Fort Pillow, Tennessee, with a force of 1,500 against 557 Federal soldiers, including 262 black troops. The Federals surrendered, but a massacre, especially of black troops, ensued.

The Union advance guards had been driven back to the fort at about 6 A.M. The rebels pursued with skirmishers and sharpshooters and fighting lasted for about two hours, with the Confederates taking over the Federal rifle pits and firing from both flanks until about noon. They then launched an attack on the Union works but were pushed back twice. The attackers demanded that the Union forces surrender. While the demand was being considered, the Union soldiers held their fire. But many of the rebels used the cease-fire to crawl closer to Union lines.

The men in the fort refused to surrender and the rebels launched a ferocious attack. The black regiment collapsed, leaving an opening for the attackers to pour into the fort. An indiscriminate slaughter followed. Union soldier Daniel H. Rankin, Company C, 13th Tennessee Cavalry Volunteers, took off his cartridge box and asked for mercy. He heard a Confederate officer order his men to kill the prisoners and show no quarter. Rankin surrendered but the attackers kept firing. He was hit seven times, although some of his wounds were light. He was taken prisoner.

Rankin saw twelve white soldiers and perhaps thirty black soldiers shot down after surrendering and while begging for mercy. He witnessed fifty defenseless blacks, who had tried to escape by wading across a nearby river, shot and killed. He saw a rebel officer attempt to save a small black boy by placing him on his horse. One of the officer's superiors yelled to him, "Take that God-damned nigger down and shoot him," or the soldier would be shot himself. The order was obeyed and the child was killed.

Hardy N. Revelle, a Union soldier, said he saw two white men of the 13th Tennessee Cavalry standing behind a stump. They had placed a white handkerchief over it and asked for mercy. When they stepped out, rebel soldiers shot and killed them. A captain of the rebel troops then came and ordered all the Federal troops, black and white, to move up the hill or he would "shoot their . . . brains out."

One Union soldier who escaped described the scene: "I also saw Negroes shot down with pistols in the hands of rebels. One was killed at my side. I saw another Negro struck on the head with a saber by a rebel soldier. I suppose he was also killed. One more just in front of me was knocked down with the butt of a musket. We kept on up the hill. I expected each moment to meet my fate with the rest." The soldier saw Sandy Sherman, of Company D, 6th U. S. Heavy Artillery, murdered in cold blood.

Anne Jane Rufins, whose husband was a member of the 13th Tennessee Cavalry, said she saw the remains of a man lying upon his back, with his arms outstretched and planks under him. "The man had to all appearances been nailed to the side of the house, and then the building set on fire," Rufus said. "I am satisfied that the body was that of Lt. John C. Ackerstrom, second lieutenant Company A, Thirteenth Tennessee Cavalry, who was on duty as quartermaster of the post of Fort Pillow. I was well acquainted with Lt. Ackerstrom when living."

The Union lost 231 killed, 100 wounded, and 226 taken prisoner. The Confederates lost 14, with 86 wounded.

The headline in the *New York Herald* reported: MASSACRE OF THE WHITE AND BLACK TROOPS, WOMEN AND CHILDREN MURDERED IN COLD BLOOD, THE DEAD AND WOUNDED NEGROES BURNED. The story below the headline detailed the horrors: "Both white and black were bayoneted, shot or sabered. Even dead bodies were horribly mutilated and children of seven and eight years and several Negro women killed in cold blood. Soldiers unable to speak from wounds were shot dead and their bodies rolled down the banks into the river. The dead and wounded Negroes were piled in heaps and burned, and several citizens who had joined our forces for our protection were killed or wounded."

For black soldiers, the newspaper reports were a sobering reminder of the dangers they faced on the battlefield. They could never surrender or be taken prisoner. If captured, they could not expect mercy or to be treated as prisoners of war.

The massacre ignited a deep rage in black soldiers, who promised to exact revenge. Nine days after the massacre at Fort Pillow, a black guard shot and killed a white prisoner under suspicious circumstances. For black soldiers, the war was becoming increasingly personal.

And as the war progressed, "Remember Fort Pillow" would become a rallying cry as powerful as any in the conflict that had torn the nation apart.

EIGHT

TO THE FRONT

Storming Petersburg

If Confederate leaders lacked signs of Grant's intentions in April 1864, they merely needed to read the Northern newspapers. Profiles of Union generals with details of their coming assignments were featured within the pages of their hometown newspapers. Even society page editors seemed fully apprised of Grant's plans.

One curious reader was General Robert E. Lee, whose main army was camped in the wilderness of Virginia, north of Richmond. A flag-of-truce boat exchanged Northern and Southern newspapers every week for commanders to read about their counterparts. "I see it stated in the Northern papers that General Gilmore has been assigned a part in the proposed campaign in Virginia," Lee wrote in a dispatch.

Grant's plan to launch an attack in Virginia was the worst-kept secret in America that spring. Everyone knew it was coming; the only question was when. Speculation among the ranks led to disappointment and false alarms as the weather warmed without orders to march against the main rebel army. Soldiers bored by the war hoped for a speedy conclusion that would allow them to return home. The minor battles and expeditions that spring, such as the expeditions to free prisoners at Libby, had been halfhearted and poorly planned and not part of any grand coordinated effort. Many soldiers felt it was time to strike a decisive, fatal blow to the Confederacy with all the might Union forces could muster.

The delays were especially frustrating for black soldiers. Their battle to win respect was only half achieved. Brass buttons were not enough, as Frederick Douglass had believed, to gain admiration. Honor would have to be earned in battle.

They had marched more than a hundred miles in four days during Wistar's strike against Richmond. Yet the hardship of that feat earned them only a demeaning backhanded compliment. Black soldiers were fine for marching, but not for winning battles, was the prevailing conventional wisdom. Black soldiers had shown valor in defeat against impossible odds at Fort Wagner, Olustee, and Fort Pillow. But those battles were defeats nevertheless.

Wistar, who had initially doubted black troops' ability to march, now questioned their ability to fight. He turned back his expedition in February rather than send the black regiments against the battery near Richmond. When General Butler decided to reorganize the officers in his command, he offered Wistar a black regiment. Wistar hesitated in part because he believed black soldiers were unreliable in battle. But faced with the prospect of missing out on the upcoming campaign, he reluctantly took command of the regiment.

Now he and his black troops waited impatiently for their orders. The delays in military action that so frustrated the troops were partly political. Handing over the reins of the Union army from General George Meade to General Ulysses S.

Grant meant a Senate confirmation. The war effort became hostage to Congress's calendar. The Senate voted to revive the rank of lieutenant general in late February to give Grant full command of the Union army. He was confirmed in early March.

Grant traveled to Washington to accept the commission, among hoopla and great expectations. He quietly checked into the Willard Hotel accompanied by his fourteen-year-old son. The clerk didn't recognize the small, unimposing man with the weary look in his eye of a longtime drinker and said only a less luxurious top-floor room was available. Grant nodded that he would take it. Only after Grant scratched his signature on the registry did the clerk recognize the highly lauded hero. The best room in the hotel was provided. Guests whispered Grant's name with near reverence as he sat in the dining room. Finally shouts and cheers went up before the patrons allowed the newly minted lieutenant general to eat in peace.

Grant spent a week in Washington attending the ceremonies and parties held in his honor. It was the very week that Fleetwood, Holland, Hawkins, Veal, and the black regiments marched to King and Queen County in Virginia to avenge Lieutenant Dahlgren's ambush.

Ceremonies behind him, Grant quickly went about developing a new strategy for the war. He met with President Lincoln on March 24 to lay out his plan. It called for the launching of a series of massive coordinated attacks to keep constant pressure on Lee and his armies. Grant's ultimate goal was the taking of Richmond, an act that most believed would signal the end of the conflict.

The black troops were a part of Grant's equation. While not a convert to their abilities on the battlefield, he fully intended to use them in his massive push into rebel territory. Butler, under whose overall command the black troops fell, was to have control of at least twenty thousand men in the campaign. His mission was to move his troops up the James by transports and take City Point, a small signal station at the mouth of the Appomattox where the river runs into the James. The point was between Richmond and Petersburg, about fifteen miles from the capital.

"When you are notified to move, take City Point with as much force as possible," Butler's orders read. "Fortify, or rather entrench, at once, and concentrate all your troops for the field there as rapidly as you can."

City Point would be a launching pad for other operations. Grant wanted to make sure Butler held the position against a Confederate counterattack and directed that fortifications, rifle pits, and trenches be built as soon as the men landed.

Richmond was to be Butler's ultimate objective. Grant wanted his armies to move together in a coordinated attack on the city. It would be, in Grant's estimation, the massive blow to the Confederacy that the Union army longed for.

As Grant and his officers formulated their plan of attack during late March and early April, Fleetwood returned to the routine of camp life. It was still unpleasantly cold at times and fuel for heat, constantly in short supply around the regiment, completely ran out on some days, leaving the men scrambling to keep warm. On one really cold day, Fleetwood wrote his report from bed to avoid the cold.

On April 9, the 4th, 5th, and 6th black regiments were ordered to leave Fort Monroe for Point Lookout, where the 36th U.S. Colored Troops was already stationed. The trip, aboard the massive transports that ferried troops along the rivers, was made in a heavy downpour. The troops arrived at Point Lookout about 8 P.M., but stayed on board the vessels overnight because of the rain. Fleetwood, who had good quarters in the ship's stateroom, was pleased with the decision.

The troops began setting up camp the next day, assuming they would soon see action. But the excitement quickly evaporated as no orders for battle came. For the next two weeks, the regiments spent their time at the usual chores, guard details, drills, and dress parade.

In the meantime, Grant was finalizing plans with his commanders. He suggested that Butler send his cavalry to Hickford to cut the railroad connection between Petersburg and Richmond. Petersburg served as a warehouse and supply depot for goods going to the rebel army from the south and was critically important to the Confederacy. If the rail could be taken, Lee would be cut off from the rest of the South. The shortage of supplies would cripple his army and force him to retreat into North Carolina.

Finally on April 23, after weeks of inactivity, the black troops were reorganized in brigades in anticipation of the campaign. "In suspense waiting for orders," an excited Fleetwood noted. Everyone was eager to move out. They didn't have long to wait. The troops were ferried to join the thousands of troops converging at Fort Monroe. The men were in good spirits, drinking beer and singing under a warm spring sky dotted by thousands of stars.

They arrived at Fort Monroe and marched to nearby Camp Hamilton. The area was swarming with tens of thousands of troops from all over the country. Fleetwood visited the 6th, where Hawkins and Kelly were stationed. He ate dinner and slept there among his friends. That night, thousands of soldiers slept in the open on stretchers that seemed to extend for miles. It was difficult not to get caught up in the moment—the great army of the North was coming together and black soldiers were finally a part of it.

But the black troops were hardly considered equals. Reminders of this were everywhere. They were in segregated units, barred from becoming officers, paid less than their white counterparts, and given inferior weapons.

On April 29, Fleetwood received a new revolver and was nearly shot when it malfunctioned. The incident underlined a major concern already on the minds of some Union commanders regarding the reliability of firearms given to black soldiers. General Edward Hinks, who was in Camp Hamilton that day, wrote Butler complaining about the quality of the weapons blacks carried. He raised the specter of another Fort Pillow, at the time a two-week-old raw memory, in presenting his case.

"In view of the approaching campaign, and more especially on account of the recent inhumanities of the enemy perpetrated upon troops of like character to those of my command, I deem it my duty to urge that these troops shall be more efficiently armed, to enable them to defend themselves and lessen their liability to capture," the general argued. "There certainly ought to be no objection to arming these troops with as effective a weapon as any that are placed in the hands of white soldiers, who are to go into battle with none of the peculiar disadvantages to which my men will be subject."

Hinks said the rifled muskets in the hands of black troops were inferior to those given to whites. The Springfield rifled muskets of the Bridesburg manufacture and the Enfields carried by blacks had well-documented histories of failure in the field. Some soldiers carried the even older Harpers Ferry smoothbore.

"[Since the black troops] cannot afford to be beaten, and will not be taken, the best arm should be given that the country can afford. The retaliation we should at present adopt is to arm our colored troops with Spencer repeating rifles, and I request that my division, or a part of them, may be armed with a repeating or breech-loading firearm."

Hinks's request was noted by superiors and ignored. The

black soldiers would fight much of the war as poorly armed as when they entered the service.

On May 1, the black regiments were ordered to prepare for light marching. "Much excitement prevalent," Fleetwood jotted in his journal. More than sixty steamers had arrived near the camp. Moving preparations continued Monday as the men pared down their belongings. Overcoats and extra clothing were shipped to storage in Norfolk. The men planned to take little more than their clothes and weaponry. Fleetwood went to the store with Handy to pick up some items. Later, they visited two young ladies they had befriended, Misses Williams and Dashields. The women were concerned about the upcoming battle, but Fleetwood downplayed the danger and promised to return to see them when the expedition was over.

They were to leave that day, but in the afternoon a furious storm swept in off the sea with driving wind and rain. It lasted two hours and blew the tents so hard that the men struggled to keep them from blowing away. The storm guaranteed the postponement of the campaign for at least one more day, and the men cursed their luck. Fleetwood noted that the delay left the regiment "much disgruntled."

As the troops waited impatiently in camp the following day, black soldiers had a rare reason to celebrate when it was announced that Congress had just adjusted their pay, making it equal to that of whites. The news was met with a resounding cheer. For many black soldiers it wasn't just about the money, it was about something less tangible—self-respect.

Things were slowly coming together as Fleetwood and others hoped. First the Emancipation Proclamation, now equal pay—blacks could only hope that their willingness to sacrifice their lives would bring the full benefits of citizenship they so desperately craved.

The men finally boarded the transports headed for City Point on May 2, and the boats steamed up the river in a long fleet that stretched as far as eye could see, their signal lights flashing like commanders winking at each other in secret code. A fleet of gunboats led the convoy up the James River. Milton and the 5th were in the rear boats, just in front of the steamers carrying General Hinks and General Butler.

To onlookers along the shores, the great armada was a stunning sight, almost forty thousand armed troops aboard some sixty steamers heading upriver, ready for rampage. They seemed invincible. Ships and men passed Jamestown, the first settlement in Virginia. Only the ruins of a small brick church remained of the storied settlement. The men were not ignorant to the history before their eyes.

"Many things attracted our attention along the banks of the James, too numerous to mention," mused the ex-slave Holland. "One I might mention particularly, was the ruins of Jamestown, the spot where the curse of slavery was first introduced into the United States. A serpent that has inserted his poisonous fangs into the body of this government, causing it to wither in its bloom."

Soon the fleet became separated along the winding river. Butler sent a message through the signal corps back to Hinks in the rear to "crowd on all steam, and hurry up." His men, Butler felt, had a date with destiny. He had no intention of keeping the fickle lady waiting.

Hinks, who got the message to hurry up, now inquired of Admiral Lee if it was safe to proceed up the river. His concern was enemy torpedoes, underwater mines that could wreak havoc with even ironclad vessels. The admiral's response brought him some comfort: "The channel has been searched as far as City Point."

One of the Monitors ran aground as the black regiments passed Harrison's Landing at about 3 P.M., a famous spot from the Peninsula Campaign under McClellan two years earlier.

As they steamed along the James, the men saw the steeples of Petersburg just seven miles to the southwest; Richmond lay about fifteen miles to the north. Both cities seemed within their grasp and they could imagine victory by nightfall and the war would be over. Nearing the area, the men could see the Confederate signal officers frantically relaying word of the approaching Union forces. The flashing lights screamed the warning across the horizon.

The fleet landed a number of the black soldiers at Wilson's Wharf, which they quickly seized. They captured the signal tower after rebel officers fled in fright. Their landing seemed to be a complete surprise to the enemy. The convoy steamed ahead to Fort Powhatan, where two more of Wild's regiments disembarked on shore and chased a small group of rebels off.

By evening, Holland and the rest of the black troops under Colonel Samuel A. Duncan could see City Point, where they were scheduled to land. It was known as an exchange point for prisoners and consisted of about a half dozen houses on the high bluff of a bank, situated just below the conflux of the James and Appomattox rivers. As the transports neared the city, Company C of the 6th U.S. Colored Infantry was ordered ashore. Milton and the others marched up a hill where a Confederate flag was posted. They tore it down and hoisted a Union flag in its place. "The flag of the glorious free could be seen floating in the breeze," Holland noted with pride. Then a crimson battle flag was run up the halyards. "As it was unfolded by the breeze and its three glittering stars sparkled in the bright sunlight, it was greeted by thundering cheers by our men," Scroggs noted.

As the soldiers pushed forward they encountered only light

opposition, quickly capturing forty prisoners and chasing away several rebels. One platoon chased the retreating rebels a short distance before letting up and returning to camp. All was going as planned.

An obviously pleased Butler messaged Grant an update of his troops' activities: "No opposition thus far. Apparently a complete surprise."

The rebels were spread too thin to present any serious threat to Butler's men. Fewer than ten thousand Confederates were positioned in a fifty-mile area around Richmond and Petersburg to oppose the Army of the James, which now numbered about forty thousand. The bulk of the Confederate army was battling the Army of the Potomac north of Richmond in one of the costliest campaigns of the war.

Petersburg was particularly vulnerable, but Butler hesitated to take advantage of the mismatch, and the heavy action the black soldiers hoped to see didn't materialize. Instead, Butler placed his men in a holding pattern, building entrenchments and fortifications. It was a moment for decisive leadership and the general showed himself lacking in that department.

Scroggs expressed the disappointment that ran through the ranks of the black regiments: "I am afraid there has been a fine opportunity for decided advantages lost here by inexcusable tardiness. I will always be of the opinion that on the night on which we landed at City Point, Petersburg could have been taken without serious trouble by our division alone. Our arrival here was entirely unexpected and they were comparatively destitute of both men and arms. We lay here four days without advancing a step, and then on making a feeble attempt yesterday we found them prepared for us. Very courteous in us not to take them unawares."

Fleetwood, Holland, and others in their regiments worked

putting up fortifications to repel a counterattack by the enemy. Butler reported that the earthworks around City Point were progressing well. Heavy guns, including a thirty-pounder, two twenty-pounders, and one eight-inch howitzer, were being mounted.

The black soldiers worked and waited, an all-too-familiar pattern. From a distance they watched the flashing signal lights from various Union positions up and down the river, some bringing news from as far away as Washington and President Lincoln.

Over the next several days the black troops would hear—and in some cases see—fighting in the distance but played little or no role in it. Even when the order came to advance against the rebels' Richmond-Petersburg line of communication, the black soldiers were placed a safe distance from the front, their combat experience relegated to minor skirmishes and limited excursions.

The men had marched sixteen miles without firing a shot. Some began to openly complain about being left out of the major battles. As news continued to arrive about the bloody fights north of Richmond, the troops became more frustrated.

Part of the problem, as many saw it, was a lack of faith in the black troops. They had often been placed at the point of attack in the first line of battle. But when their commanders had been given the choice of charging or retreating, most chose to retreat.

Colonel Duncan's black regiments weren't the only black troops frustrated on the sidelines of the war. Back at Point Lookout, the 36th U.S. Colored Troops, which included Gardiner and James, was also removed from the heavy fighting. Relegated to guarding rebel prisoners, members of the regiment welcomed an assignment to seek and destroy Confederate underwater mines.

On May 11, three hundred men from the 36th took part in a minesweeping operation to the mouth of the Rappahannock. The men prodded the river and quickly found five torpedoes. They exploded three and raised the other two. Union sympathizers in the area identified local mill owner Henry Barrack as having helped place the mines. The black troops marched to Barrack's mill and burned it to the ground. In a continued sweep of the area, the soldiers came upon nine rebel troops, led by B. G. Burley and John Maxwell of the Confederate navy.

The black soldiers, separated from their officers, didn't wait for orders to engage the enemy. A fight erupted and shots echoed across the swamp. The soldiers soon received backup and succeeded in killing or capturing almost the entire rebel party, except for one man who escaped. Maxwell and four others were killed. Burley, a sergeant, and a cavalry corporal were captured. The black soldiers suffered four casualties, including one man killed. Another was only slightly wounded. But the excitement of the soldiers ran high and the fight almost ended in the murder of the captives. Some of the black soldiers wanted vengeance for the cruel slaughter at Fort Pillow a month earlier. But one soldier, Sergeant Price, urgently pleaded with the men to stop the bloodshed.

"This little affair was conducted wholly by the black men as no officers arrived until after the fight was over," Colonel Alonzo Draper reported. "The colored soldiers would have killed all the prisoners had they not been restrained by Sergeant Price, who is also colored."

Meanwhile, after an engagement with rebel forces, Butler boasted that his men had completely thwarted the enemy south of Richmond. "That portion which reached Petersburg under Hill I have whipped to-day, killing and wounding many and taking many prisoners, after a severe and well-contested fight.

General Grant will not be troubled with any further reinforcements to Lee from Beauregard's force."

But he was sadly mistaken.

Confederate president Davis worried as Butler's army
moved closer to Petersburg and Drewry's Bluff. Any interruption to the railroad line would endanger the capital and cut Lee
off from the rest of the South. Davis sent Lee a message to
underline his concerns: "Affairs here are critical." Davis
diverted all the troops he could to Virginia to stall Butler's army.
Rebel soldiers came pouring into the area from South Carolina,
Georgia, and parts of Florida.

General Beauregard's ten rebel brigades crept out of the
early morning fog at 4 A.M. on May 16 to attack the Army of the
James at Drewrey's Bluff. Fleetwood watched the fighting on
the Federal right, where General Baldy Smith's troops suffered
heavy casualties. The men of the 5th—Beaty, Bronson, Holland, and Pinn—could see the battle unfolding to the left,
where General Quincy A. Gillmore's troops were entrenched.
Butler's army withdrew completely from the area the next day,
pushed back by Beauregard. In the end, the Confederates held
the railroad.

The black regiments of the 4th, 5th, and 6th had remained
strangely removed from the fighting. Fleetwood watched the
fighting from a bluff. Some of the soldiers rode skiffs on the
James to pass the time. The constant boom of artillery fire and
the rattle of small arms were reminders that war was just a few
miles away.

While savage fighting continued north of Richmond, the
black regiments waited. Fleetwood was still lying in the trenches
at City Point on Saturday, May 14, writing letters. His friend
Handy had stopped speaking to him over a misunderstanding
involving hardtack biscuits. Fleetwood had fried and eaten

three pieces; Handy thought his friend should have shared at least one piece, but didn't. The two men hadn't spoken in days, and Handy had demanded that Fleetwood leave his tent.

Life was miserable in the trenches, where the men were stationed every other day. The wet weather left the ravines muddy and uncomfortable. Many of the troops remained irritated that they hadn't gone into battle.

On Wednesday, May 18, Fleetwood spent the early part of the morning watching a Federal gunboat shell the rebels. The weather turned cloudy and it began to rain. He was heading back to his tent to dry out when the regiment was called out double quick. The Confederates were advancing toward City Point.

At 11 A.M. the rebels attacked from the Petersburg Road. A heavy shelling of the reserve of the 4th's grand guard began. Two Confederate squadrons of cavalry appeared. The riders moved into line near two pieces of artillery. Rebel skirmishers were spotted coming up the roads along the woods to the front of the Union position. Another group of enemy horsemen appeared on the left of the line.

The rebel battery launched some shots to the Union right. The soldiers were forced to fall back, and enemy fire came whistling forward. But the men didn't panic. They withdrew a few feet and returned fire, taking time to aim carefully and send purposeful shots at the enemy.

As the rebels pressed forward, Union soldiers opened up with the big Federal guns. Navy gunboats along the river also fired on the rebels. For half an hour, the booming sounds of cannons echoed, finally forcing the Confederates to withdraw. Most of the rebels were cavalry, making pursuit by foot soldiers useless.

Duncan believed the rebels had suffered heavy casualties.

They had been caught in the crossfire of the gunboats at a distance of just a thousand yards. Two men from the 4th were wounded. "Johnny reb woke us with a few shells. Got his answer and left," Fleetwood noted dryly. After the excitement, he relaxed by singing. He listened to a band that had been brought in to entertain the troops and then crawled into bed under changing weather. The choirmaster turned soldier was adjusting to military life far better than even he had expected.

The black regiments spent the next week in relative peace, sheltered from the fighting that surrounded them. Grant's and Lee's armies were fighting at Spotsylvania north of Richmond on Thursday, May 19. Many of the soldiers complained bitterly about the missed opportunity to take Petersburg when they first landed. "What could have been easily accomplished on our first arrival at this point of moving directly against the enemy's position is now only done by hard fighting and heavy losses," Scroggs noted.

Fleetwood and his fellow soldiers continued to erect defenses at City Point and Spring Hill, within earshot of the constant boom of cannons and artillery from the gunboats, as well as the crack of rifle fire. Fleetwood spent part of the day on picket duty and then read Captain Eberhardt's copy of *Harper's*. Later, he went for a swim, and could hear the pounding roar of cannons to the north. He joined friends to sing until 11 P.M. and then retired. It was a surreal life as one of the war's bloodiest conflicts raged just miles from camp.

For black soldiers, the first month of the Richmond-Petersburg expedition had amounted to little more than skirmishes, the digging of entrenchments, the building of fortifications, and marathon marches. That was about to change.

Grant decided to change his strategy and secretly move his one hundred thousand men from Cold Harbor outside

Richmond to a spot occupied by the black troops outside Petersburg. To confuse General Lee, he feigned a movement toward Richmond while his army crossed the James. His headquarters would be City Point, the spot captured by the black soldiers of Holland's regiment. While the Army of the Potomac moved south, General Butler and the black troops were ordered to storm Petersburg to keep as many Confederates busy as possible.

On June 14, the soldiers prepared for a coordinated attack on enemy fortifications outside of Petersburg. Previous attempts on the city had been halfhearted and timid, although at one time Butler had been ordered to take the city with bayonet, if necessary. Now the preparations for an impending assault were evident. On Sunday, the 5th U.S. Colored Troops finally got its long-awaited chaplain. The following day the troops were issued whiskey. Both were unmistakable signs that combat was imminent.

When the marching orders came, the men were instructed to pack two days' rations. They pulled up camp near Point of Rocks and crossed the Appomattox by pontoon bridge near City Point, where it meets the James River. They camped that night near Spring Hill, and slept beneath rubber blankets. Baldy Smith's division had the advance detail. His men crossed the Appomattox at Point of Rocks. Straw and hay were placed on the floating bridge to deaden the sound of the troops crossing the river.

At 1 A.M. the black regiments rose and began the march to Petersburg. They moved through the darkness among a sea of thousands of troops crossing paths in the night for the beginning of the assault. The black regiments halted to allow the 1st and 2nd divisions of the 18th Corps to pass. The black brigade, comprised of the 4th, 5th, 6th, and 22nd Colored Troops, totaled about 2,200 able-bodied fighting men that morning. They were accompanied by several white regiments, including the 5th Massachusetts Cavalry, Holman's brigade of 1,300 offi-cers and men, Angel's battery of the 136th, and Choate's black battery of the 111th. The force totaled 3,747 men.

They moved out again at about 5 A.M., after General Kautz's cavalry had passed. Three miles from Broadway, where the Union forces were to meet Smith, the rebels began firing on them from Baylor's Farm about a mile in the distance, near the swampy area around Perkinson's Saw Mill. General Kautz's cavalry galloped off on reconnaissance to locate the rebel posi-tion and gauge the size of Beauregard's force.

The black troops would lead the charge. Duncan's brigade was formed on the first line, Holman's in the second. As the men gathered into position, they were given ample time to consider the dangers before them. They waited as the 5th Mass-achusetts Cavalry, which was composed of new recruits, awkwardly moved into line.

In the early morning light, Fleetwood, Veal, Hawkins, Kelly, Beaty, and the others could see a gauntlet of obstacles. The rebels had bunkered down behind quickly made rifle pits on a crest of a hill about a thousand yards away. The first six hundred yards consisted of a densely wooded area; the remainder was across an open field in full view of the hill where the rebels waited securely entrenched.

Even raw recruits appreciated the danger. The Confederates would have a chance to fire on them as they fought their way through a tangle of underbrush in the woods. A turnpike ran through the woods and a railroad line intersected it. These obstacles would tend to delay the advance and cause breaks in the lines even before they confronted the enemy. Furthermore, the floor of the woods, marshy and strewn with fallen timbers, was covered with a dense thicket of vines and bushes that reached twenty feet high.

Surveying the scene, Colonel Duncan felt the fortifications were intimidating. "A hastily constructed earth-work with a connected line of rifle-pits, crossing the road at right angles and running along the crest nearly parallel to the outline of the wood, added much to the natural strength of the position, and rendered the enemy's occupation of this point a serious obstacle to farther progress. Behind this parapet the enemy was posted with four pieces of artillery and a considerable force of infantry."

For many in the black regiments, including Fleetwood and Hilton, Veal, Bronson, Pinn, and the others, this would be their first real combat experience, their moment of truth. As McMurray put it, "We had considerable experience in marching, some in throwing up earthworks, and were fairly well trained in company regimental, and brigade drill, but in fighting we were novices. But now we were at the turning point, and from this time forward, we were destined to experience our full share of vicissitudes of war."

The brigade was formed in front of the woods. General Hinks explained to the men that their mission was to march through the brush and take the enemy fortifications. Colonel Conine and the 5th were on the right. The 22nd, under Colonel Joseph B. Kiddoo, was on the right center; the 4th, under Colonel Rogers, was at the left center; and the 6th, under Colonel Ames, was on the left. Orders were issued to each regimental commander, who passed them to the troops. The first line was to open a heavy fire on the enemy upon reaching the farther skirt of the woods and reestablish the battle line as quickly as possible after passing through the series of obstacles. Then they would wait for an order to charge.

As the men began to move forward toward the wooded area, the enemy's battery opened a furious shelling of the dense brush, inflicting considerable damage. Trees splintered and men fell under the relentless fire. Wounded men screamed in pain as a hailstorm of enemy fire ripped through the ranks. The wood and swamp and creek proved difficult obstacles to cross. Still, the men pushed on, fighting through the six hundred yards of brush. The rebels bore down with cannon fire, heavy artillery, and muskets along the whole line. The 4th Regiment with Fleetwood, Hilton, and Veal was the first to reach the open field. In the excitement, the center companies cheered in adrenaline-induced excitement and charged up the hill without forming their lines.

Colonel Rogers, realizing the men were heading for a useless slaughter if disorganized, screamed frantically for the men to return to the cover of the woods. This attracted the attention of Beauregard's troops, who opened fire with destructive canisters from their big guns. To make matters worse, the 5th Massachusetts began firing wildly into the 4th U.S. Colored Infantry.

"The inexperience of the troops, the terrible fire to which they were subjected, and the nature of ground caused no little confusion among them, which was much increased by the second line in the excitement of the moment opening fire upon the first line," Colonel Duncan noted.

Captain King was killed and Captains Mendall and Parrington and Lieutenant Brigham were wounded. Brigham's injury proved fatal. One hundred fifty men out of six hundred from the 4th were killed. Fleetwood saw men fall around him.

The 6th Regiment with Hawkins and Kelly moved quickly through the trees and brush. But in the early morning darkness they overlapped and became entangled with the 4th. On reaching the edge of the woods the 6th was hit by fire from the left. The men prepared for a charge, but the brigade's line was too torn up to make an immediate advance.

Yet the right side of the line took advantage of the diversion of fire to the left and formed a regular battle line. Colonel Kiddoo waited for orders for his 22nd Colored Infantry to charge. He was concerned that the rough terrain would prevent an order to advance from reaching him, or that his regiment would not be found. He couldn't remain stationary because the rebel guns had begun shelling his troops. So he lined his men up for the advance. Holland and others from the 5th U.S. Colored Infantry were also in the line of enemy fire.

"We were then in the open field, halted, where we kept up a brisk fire on the skirmish line until the regiments could get through the swamps and form in order again," Holland noted. "All this while the enemy poured a galling fire of musketry, grape and canister into ranks slaying many. The order was given to forward the skirmish line one hundred paces, this being done we halted, keeping up our fire along the line."

Just then, the men saw a curious sight, a rebel soldier riding a white horse while yelling loudly to exhort his men. He drew the attention of the whole Union division. "It was that brave and daring but strange personage that rides the white charger," Holland noted. "We could see him plainly riding up and down the rebel lines, could hear him shouting from the top of his voice to stand, that they had only niggers to contend with." The rider seemed oblivious to the danger from the Federal muskets. "This peculiar personage seems possessed with supernatural talent," Holland thought. "He would sometimes ride his horse with almost lightning speed, up and down his lines amid the most terrific fire of shot and shell. But when the command was given to us 'Charge bayonets! Forward double quick!' the black column rushed forward, raising the battle yell, and in a few moments more we mounted the rebel parapets."

At 8 A.M., Hinks gave the order to charge. Milton and members of the 5th and 22nd Colored Troops raced up the rising ground, yelling loudly as they came, and flooded the rebel works. The enemy had fled, abandoning a twelve-pounder gun. Black soldiers from the 22nd immediately turned it around and fired on the retreating rebels. "To our great surprise, we found that the boasted Southern chivalry had fled. They could not see the nigger part as the man on the white horse presented it," Holland sneered.

Charles Carleton Coffin, a war correspondent, witnessed the charge:

"The colored men stepped out of the woods and stood before the enemy. They gave volley, and received one in return. Shells crashed through them, but unheeding the storm with a yell they started up the slope upon the run. They received one canister, one scathing volley of musketry. Seventy of their number went down, but the living hundreds rushed on. The Rebels did not wait their coming, but fled towards Petersburg, leaving one of the pieces of artillery in the hands of assailants, who leaped over the works, turned it in a twinkling. The colored troops were wild with joy. They embraced the captured cannon with affectionate enthusiasm, patting it as if it were animate, and could appreciate the endearment. Every soldier of the colored division was two inches taller for that achievement, said an officer describing it."

Cheers went up among the men. "The charge was gallantly made," Kiddoo noted.

The black soldiers rested for about an hour and then moved on toward the strong defenses at Jordan's Field. The enemy pickets on Bailey's Creek, near Bryant's House, were driven off.

The Union troops arrived at about 10 A.M. and could see the extensive maze of fortifications protecting Richmond. "A good engineer officer had done his work well in planning this system," General Smith noted.

That engineer had been Captain Charles H. Dimmock, for

which the series of fortifications were named. The "Dimmock Line" ran a total of ten miles from ends of the Appomattox above and below the town. The batteries gave heavy guns a clear sweep of the field the troops must cross to overrun them. Each battery was connected with a six-foot barrier that allowed rebel soldiers to fire while well protected. The trenches were further protected by a ditch, six feet deep and fifteen feet across. And before that, trees had been leveled and branches sharpened to ensnare and slow advancing soldiers while rebel sharpshooters took aim.

Soldiers from the 5th U.S. Colored Regiment were sent out as skirmishers on the left of the road. They moved through a dense thicket for about a mile, positioning themselves in front of Batteries No. 6, 7, 8, 9, and 10, which were about two miles from the city. A couple of regimental companies from Beauregard's troops were driven off.

Many of the troops wondered why an attack wasn't made on the works at that moment. The rebels were working frantically to fortify the position and bring more troops to the area. Each passing minute meant the task would be more difficult and dangerous. And as the day progressed, the men would become more fatigued. But a series of mishaps had caused delays.

Smith, who had just returned from Cold Harbor, where he witnessed how well-armed entrenchments could decimate a larger advancing force, was still waiting for Major General Winfield S. Hancock's troops to arrive to double the size of their force. Hancock's men had become initially lost in the darkness, then, following poorly marked maps, had actually headed in the opposite direction. Also, Grant's confusing orders to take Petersburg only if it seemed to pose no difficulty left Smith leaning on the side of caution.

General Smith decided he needed to find a weakness in the

fortifications. But he didn't have an engineer officer, as his request for one had been denied the night before. The task was left to him. It was slow work. He not only had to juggle his duties as the commander of the attack with his surveying chores, but he also battled the effects of illness. The water at Cold Harbor had brought on a serious case of dysentery, which was raging. He could hardly sit on his horse. Exposure to sunlight for more than a few minutes resulted in an intense headache. As he emerged from different vantage points from the woods to view the rebel fortifications, the enemy would launch shells and musket fire in his direction.

Colonel Duncan sent his black troops to the edge of surrounding woods that flanked the batteries, which held a commanding position over the entire field before them. He instructed the men that they were to fire into the batteries in an effort to silence the guns while his army charged. The men moved quietly through the patch of woods to the farthest edge. But this left them six hundred yards short of the batteries and too far to drive the rebels from the works. Between the blue-coated soldiers and the batteries lay open, exposed ground. Duncan decided it would be safer to wait for dusk to move forward. "Furthermore, any advance of the regiment beyond this point would have separated it from all support from the rest of the command, which was to be advanced in a different direction," he concluded.

Meanwhile the artillery regiments tried firing on the works from an open field to near the right and rear of his regiment. But the enemy's guns sent them scrambling. Duncan withdrew the artillery.

Hinks ordered a double line of battle formed: the 4th Regiment with Fleetwood, Veal, and Hilton on the right and the 22nd on the left of the first line, and the 5th with Beaty,

Bronson, Pinn, and Holland on the right and the 6th with Hawkins and Kelly on the left of the second line. The 1st U.S. Colored Troops, under the command of Lieutenant Colonel Elias Wright, connected with the left of the first line.

The order to charge went up. With a loud yell, the men ran in quick strides five hundred yards forward to a small crest in Jordan's Field. Enemy fire from three sides came raining down on them. The Union artillery guns, which had moved well to the rear, opened fire to provide cover for the advancing troops, their shells whistling above the men as they ran. Even for the fastest men in the regiments, the run to the nearest cover took a full minute. By 2 P.M., most of the men were crowded in the field, where they were forced to lie for the next five hours.

The rebels never slowed their fire, sending canisters in the direction of the sea of blue troops. Shells exploded above the men. Lead balls the size of hickory nuts and sharp metal fell like rain on them. The troops had no way to protect themselves. It was a dangerous, frightening time.

Lieutenant Jones, a white officer of Company A of the 6th U.S. Colored Troops, became frantic over the spherical shells exploding around him. Every time a shell burst and one of its fragments hit him, he would move to a spot he thought was safer. He jumped from spot to spot until a little iron ball came down on him, tearing into his ankle from inside his shoe top. The ball ripped through his tendon, leaving him screaming in pain.

Captain McMurray was talking with a soldier from a white regiment when he turned and saw a shell bounding toward him. He leaped frantically out of its path, but watched in horror as it instantly killed the other man almost in midsentence.

General Smith's hopes of a quick cavalry strike vanished when he heard artillery fire in the distance. The riders were unable to get close. "This seemed to make it more imperative that I should make no failure with the infantry and therefore made my examination the more close."

After several hours, Smith decided an infantry column advance would draw the fire of the heavy guns and demoralize the troops. Instead, he opted to send heavy skirmish lines that would be too thinly spread for cannon fire to be effective. If the rebels had not manned the fortifications with a large force of infantry, the skirmishers could infiltrate the batteries. He rode to Hinks and explained his strategy. The black troops would be sent to make an advance. Smith ordered the artillery to open fire on the enemy at any cost to provide cover fire for the foot soldiers. But to his shock, the chief of artillery had sent his horses out for water. This delayed any possible attack for two hours, from 5 P.M. to 7 P.M.

Smith sent word to Hinks at about 5 P.M. that he planned to order a charge on the Confederate works. He wanted the troops to move into position for the attack. When General William B. Brooks's line moved forward, the black regiments were to charge and dislodge in all the enemy's sharpshooters.

Butler's signal corps reported that trains of troops had left Richmond and were headed for Petersburg. He sent a message to Grant at 5:20 P.M. that Petersburg was being reinforced. "The lookout at the signal station on the right just reports that clouds of dust are seen on the north side of the James, seeming to be caused by two brigades of infantry and about 200 wagons and ambulances crossing Chaffin's farm."

Three companies of the 4th U.S. Colored Infantry under Major Borenstein, Fleetwood's direct superior, moved to the woods to reinforce the skirmishers at 5:30 P.M. Four companies from the 22nd U.S. Colored Troops joined them under Major Cook. They were ordered to charge from the woods to the works as soon as they saw the right side of the brigade advance under Brooks. The rebel sharpshooters had been driven back by the skirmish line. They stood in the woods watching the battle line closely, adjusting and readjusting their weapons.

As soon as Brooks moved forward, the 4th and 22nd sprinted from the woods, yelling loudly as they advanced. Colonel Joseph B. Kiddoo of the 22nd watched them, hoping they could outrun danger. The men "cheerfully obeyed this order and advanced on the run till they got so far under the guns of the battery as to be sheltered from their fire," he said. The Union batteries had been moved into place and unleashed a bombardment over the head of the charging soldiers. Holland noted, "It is useless for me to attempt a description of that evening cannonading. I have never heard anything to equal it before or since for a while whole batteries discharge their contents into the rebel ranks at once, the result was complete success." The men had no idea how many rebels lay in the rifle pits and trenches connecting the batteries. The Confederates opened fire, but most of their bullets went over the head of the coming tide of blue. The black troops swarmed the first line of works and found the enemy had fled. Reserves of the 4th and 22nd, which had been kept out of canister range, were ordered forward under their respective commanders to support the skirmishes.

Colonel Kiddoo, passing into the works at Battery No. 7, reestablished his lines. The 1st Regiment pushed ahead to Battery No. 8, which was posted high on a difficult ravine. They encountered a group of rebels in the trenches between the batteries and a skirmish erupted. Kiddoo decided to use the fight as a diversion for an advance by his men, who headed for Battery No. 8.

The rebels abandoned the battery and climbed down into

the rifle pits to shoot at the advancing Union troops. They fired heavily on the men as they climbed the works, causing considerable casualties. "My men wavered at first under the hot fire of the enemy, but soon, on seeing their colors on the opposite side of the ravine, pushed rapidly up and passed the rifle pits," Kiddoo remembered.

Lieutenant Colonel Wright and the 1st U.S. Colored Infantry came up to support the soldiers climbing the works. The enemy retreated, leaving a twelve-pounder howitzer, which the men turned on the next work, Battery No. 9.

Fleetwood, Holland, and the men of the 4th and 6th followed the 22nd to Battery No. 8. Then the men ran toward Battery No. 9, about six hundred yards away, which posed a deadly threat since it had command of the batteries already taken by the Union soldiers.

Duncan called up his second line, which swung about and moved to the front of 9, 10, and 11. The works were now flooded with soldiers from the black regiments. General Smith appeared on the field and began leading the assault. A column was formed. The men from the 6th Regiment led the charge, followed by the 5th in the second line. Skirmishers were thrown out to provide cover fire, and the advance began. The Union artillery was ordered to come up and support the attack. The 22nd ran out of ammunition and fell back to a rear position.

The rest of the men had to cross six hundred yards of obstructions that included burning stumps, piles of wood, fallen timber, brushes, and small pools. By then, darkness was falling. They could see the direction of the Confederate guns by the flashes from the enemy fire. The column advanced over the hazards as best it could, with only occasional shots coming from the enemy. The rebels concentrated their fire on the storming parties advancing up the flank. "As we went forward, we came to black burnt logs as high as our breasts, sometimes climbing over them and sometimes going under. As we neared the battery, or fort, we could see that it looked grim and formidable in the dusk of the evening. But all before us was silent as death," one soldier recounted.

Finally, the men got through the slashed and blackened logs. They straightened their line, only to encounter a defensive line of felled, sharpened trees in front of the ditch that ran around the fortification. They found it strange that the enemy's guns were silent and few shots were now being fired in their direction. They feared that the rebels were waiting until they were just a few feet away to open an attack.

In minutes, the ditch in front of Battery No. 10 was full of men, who began to climb up the face of the parapet. "A man would run his bayonet into the side of the parapet, and another would use it as a step-ladder to climb up," McMurray said. "As we were ascending, I was wondering why the Johnnies behind the parapet were so quiet. It was getting quite dark, and I felt sure that as fast as a 'colored troop' would put his head above the level of that parapet it would be shot off, or he would be knocked back into the ditch; and I fully expected the Sixth U.S. Colored Troops, officers and all, to find their death in that ditch. But they didn't. Not bit of it." The rebels had fled at the sight of thousands of advancing Union soldiers. The troops climbed the battery only to find it empty, save one fair-haired rebel soldier who sat dead. He looked to be just seventeen years old. The men let out a cheer and then could hear more shouts coming from Battery No. 11, which was now in Union hands. It was now nine o'clock. The brigade was re-formed and rested for the night near Battery 10.

Smith weighed the option of whether to push the advance

toward Petersburg, but decided against it. "By this time darkness had set in, and having learned some time before that re-enforcements were rapidly coming in from Richmond, and deeming that I held important points of the enemy's line of work, I thought it prudent to make no farther advance, and made my dispositions to hold what I already had."

As news of the battle reached the high command, there seemed reason to celebrate. Butler sent a message to Grant: "Lieutenant Davenport, acting as my secretary, has just returned from General Smith's front. He holds a line of from two miles to the left of the Jordan Point road to the Appomattox, five miles in all. I have sent him back word to again push on to the Appomattox. General Hancock's corps has probably joined him ere this. They were about five miles from him at 9.30 and were advancing. General Smith has captured 13 guns and 230 prisoners. We have reason to believe that the enemy in this front has been re-enforced, and we have made every disposition to hold our own here."

Despite the heroics of the black regiments, Grant's attack on Petersburg had failed. It was an all-or-nothing venture. Smith's decision to halt the advance soon came under question. It was later learned that Beauregard had the use of just three thousand troops for most of the day. Yet the small but persistent force stopped sixteen thousand Federals. Confusion in orders, bad maps, delays by commanders, mistakes by fresh troops let precious hours of opportunity pass. As night fell, gray-coated troops poured into Petersburg, reinforcing the thin ranks. By sunrise, it was apparent that the opportunity was gone.

As the black troops formed picket lines around midnight, they could hear the rebels working frantically. They were told these were A. P. Hill's troops arranging the defenses for the city. "Twelve hours earlier, General Smith could have marched into

Petersburg at will," McMurray wrote. "Now, Grant's whole army was unable to force its way in."

By the morning, Petersburg would be an entrenched fortress and the siege of June 15 would be listed as a failure. Grant's maneuver from Cold Harbor had deceived Lee for days, but he was unable to take advantage of the sleight of hand.

But overall failure of the siege couldn't obscure the gallantry displayed by the black troops. They had withstood combat of the deadliest kind and had been cool under fire. The cost in casualties gave some indication of the danger the men faced. Of 2,200 men under Colonel Samuel Duncan's command, 391 had been killed, wounded, captured, or were missing. Of the 600 men in Fleetwood's regiment, 15 were killed and 120 wounded. The 5th suffered 41 casualties, four of them fatalities. The 6th lost 76, and the 22nd 138. Most importantly, the black soldiers had been victorious. "We have a sufficient proof that colored men, when properly officered, instructed, and drilled, will make most excellent infantry of the line, and may be used as such soldiers to great advantage," General Hinks wrote in battle reports.

Fleetwood and his fellow black soldiers had finally tasted battle.

—⚬⚬⚬—

NINE

THE FOG OF WAR
The Petersburg Mine Explosion

As the black troops manned the line before Petersburg in the darkness following their triumph, replacements came from the war-scarred veterans from the vanguard of the Army of the Potomac. These men seemed nervous, edgy, hyper-alert, as if afraid a rebel soldier lay behind every tree or crest. Many appeared shell-shocked, clinging closely to their commanders. Some of the black soldiers led the white troops by the arm to posts along the line.

If these men seemed spooked, it was no small wonder. Confederates snipers had been taking potshots at them for weeks. They had just seen some of the harshest, bloodiest fighting of the war in battles at the Wilderness and the Spotsylvania Courthouse. They had witnessed the slaughter at Cold Harbor and had great respect for Johnny Reb's fighting ability.

Fleetwood, Veal, Hilton, and other black troops curled up to sleep that night in Battery No. 9, which had been manned hours earlier by rebel soldiers. Off in the darkness, they could hear Confederate soldiers frantically building entrenchments.

In the morning, the black troops were moved to the rear, where they set up camp.

News of their assault reached Washington by morning. C. A. Dana, the assistant secretary of war, telegraphed his boss: "The success of Smith last night was of the most important character. . . . General Smith says the Negro troops fought magnificently. His loss is in round numbers 750, of which 500 were among the Negroes."

Dana spent the morning touring the captured batteries with General Grant and a group of engineers. His reaction was similar to Smith's. He was impressed with the engineering of the Dimmock Line and marveled at the valor required to breach it. In another dispatch to Secretary of War Stanton, he wrote, "The works are of the very strongest kind, more difficult even to take than was Missionary Ridge, at Chattanooga. The hardest fighting was done by the black troops. The forts they stormed were, I think, the worst of all. After the affair was over General Smith went to thank them and tell them he was proud of their courage and dash. He says they cannot be exceeded as soldiers, and that hereafter he will send them in a difficult place as readily as the best white troops."

But the newfound respect rang hollow. As McMurray, a white officer of the 6th U.S. Colored Troops put it, "General Grant didn't seem to have any use for us. He hadn't learned yet that black men were just as good fighters as white men."

Fleetwood rested most of the day following the assault. By noon, Burnside's and Warren's troops came up and most of the Army of the Potomac settled outside Petersburg after the long march from north of Richmond. In the evening, the black troops moved to the front and lay in line for about an hour, and then returned to the rear. For the next three days, fighting raged. The men spent an anxious time, oddly removed from the action. They could hear the explosion of artillery fire and the rattle of muskets. They could even hear the yells and cheers of men in the distance. Their only source of information about the fighting at the front came from the wounded or stragglers making their way back to the rear. The black troops feasted on fresh beef and rations that first night, enjoying warm and pleasant weather.

"All quiet today until turning in time when the heaviest musketry I ever heard took place," Fleetwood wrote in his diary. "Fell in manned works. Lay there all night undisturbed."

Burnside gained some ground, only to be thrown back. On Saturday, another Union charge was made through a cornfield by a division of Hancock's troops, but was turned back with heavy losses. The bitterness of the previous battles became evident when Confederate general Beauregard refused to grant permission for Union troops to remove the dead and wounded, who lay in the field several days, some in terrible agony.

Fleetwood, Veal, Hilton, and other black troops were sent to the front as reserves. They experienced heavy musket fire throughout the afternoon, finding shelter behind a hill, where Fleetwood read letters from home. Some among their ranks were killed and wounded. The next day, Fleetwood sought a safer spot. He dug a hole for shelter and lay in the field until about noon. The black troops were relieved and sent to the rear. They camped at Bermuda Hundred, where Fleetwood finally got a restful night's sleep.

By now, Grant realized that the opportunity for a thrust into Petersburg had slipped away. He had caught Lee off guard and even fooled the Southern commander about the location of his army. He had positioned a vastly superior number of troops in front of Petersburg, but had not been able to take advantage. He had traded a stalemate north of Richmond for one south of Petersburg. The city, he decided, could only be taken by a long, hard siege, much like his campaign against Vicksburg. That meant Confederate supplies would have to be cut off and the railroads to the city destroyed. But that task would take time and be costly in men. The Southerners realized their survival lay in their supply lines and would savagely defend them, a foot at a time if needed. Trenches and fortifications were built to make each foot of Union advance deadly. The fighting slowed from quick marches and galloping pursuits to agonizing trench battles, as a new, more modern type of warfare emerged.

On June 20, Fleetwood and the others got a chance to shake the dust off, wash, and change clothes. The regimental officers gave all the appearances of settling in for a stay of a week or two, Fleetwood thought. But orders to return to the front arrived late in the day. The men rose at 5 A.M. the following day, took down their tents, and packed their equipment. Fleetwood had to work alone because Handy was sick. The division crossed the river and marched toward Petersburg. Eight miles into the journey, the division halted and the men were ordered to toss all unneeded baggage. They stopped in a wooded area where their old position was visible. It was at a bluff above the railroad near the works they had captured almost a week earlier. Fleetwood took advantage of the break and napped briefly. He woke and ate. Suddenly his regiment buzzed with excitement.

A tall, gangly man, who looked to some like an undertaker, appeared. It was President Lincoln on horseback, with General Grant at his side. The soldiers cheered wildly and pressed close to the Great Emancipator. Lincoln had surprised everyone, including Grant. He had boarded a steamer the day before for a trip to inspect the lines. Earlier in that day, Grant had launched a cavalry operation against Petersburg. As he waited for news at his City Point headquarters, the commander in chief appeared, quite unannounced.

"I just thought I would jump aboard a boat and come down and see you," Lincoln told Grant matter-of-factly. "I don't expect I can do any good, and in fact I'm afraid I may do harm, but I'll just put myself under your orders and if you find me doing anything wrong just send me right away."

Grant may have wanted to do just that. But instead, he told Lincoln that he was making progress, despite appearances. Although he may have moved his army away from Richmond, the Southern capital was now in a death lock. "You will never hear of me farther from Richmond than now, till I have taken it," he told Lincoln. "I am just as sure of going into Richmond as I am of any future event. It may take a long summer day, as they say in the rebel papers, but I will do it."

Lincoln prayed Grant was right. Almost a week earlier, he had telegraphed the lieutenant general about his confidence in Grant's strategy. "I begin to see it," the president had messaged. But now he lamented the heavy future cost of lives to secure victory. "I do sincerely hope that all may be accomplished with as little bloodshed as possible," he said.

The two Union leaders rode out to view the front. It was the first day of summer, ushered in by warm and enjoyable weather. They came to the woods where General Edward Hinks's division of black soldiers had gathered as news of Lincoln's arrival spread through the ranks. One staff member described the soldiers as grinning from ear to ear. Fleetwood watched as soldiers held out their hands to touch Lincoln as his horse slowly passed. The president became overcome with emotion. He removed his famous stovepipe hat and saluted the men. Reports of their gallantry were fresh in his mind. He thanked them for their cheers.

Tears welled in his eyes. The justness of their cause stirred within their hearts deeper than ever.

Lincoln said his good-byes and rode off with Grant to thunderous cheers.

The black troops remained in the woods the next day. From their position on the high bluff, they had a panoramic view of the battle lines. Burnside's artillery could be heard to their left and the sound of skirmishing continued along the Petersburg front. At midnight, they turned out to support a battery. The Confederates launched a vigorous attack at the Union center but were quickly repulsed before the black division was needed. The morning of June 24 marked the tenth day of the siege, and was "announced by deafening artillery fire that made this earth and timid hearts quake," commented one soldier. The black troops were ordered into line at 8 A.M., where they stood until 6 P.M. before marching to Battery No. 10 in support of an attack on Petersburg. At midnight they returned to camp, where Fleetwood slept "like a brick."

In six days that followed Hancock's assault in the cornfield, the slain had lain decomposing in the field. The rebels still refused to allow a truce for the Federals to bury their dead. A detail was formed from the regiment of Thomas Hawkins and Alexander Kelly, the 6th U.S. Colored Troops, and sent out during the night to dig shallow graves to cover the bodies. "From their lines, the men could see more than a score of the dead, resting among the furrows and hillocks where the corn had grown," McMurray wrote. He counted the duty his saddest experience during the war.

The men crawled over their breastworks shortly after the sun had fallen at about ten o'clock, moving silently to avoid detection. They crept among the rows of corn, groping in the darkness for a cadaverous limb or skull while fending off scavenger animals, feeling their way along with their hands. The stench from the rotting corpses, exposed in the hot June sun for nearly a week, was almost unbearable. It was a ghastly undertaking, an apocalyptic vision. "My thoughts as I proceeded with the work were of a character that can never be described," McMurray said.

They worked within 150 yards of the enemy line. When their fingers felt a part of a dead soldier, the men began to dig a hole, keeping as quiet as possible. They rolled the corpse into the hole and blanketed it with earth. At one spot, the corpses of a group of men were discovered. Their heads were close together with their bodies extending outward like the spokes on the wheel. The gravediggers could only imagine the final moments of those men. Wounded and suffering, they had crawled to within a whisper of each other. Maybe they had talked of home, of family and friends, of the bond of eternal brotherhood among soldiers. Some may have prayed as they lay dying together.

When the last body received a proper burial, the men moved slowly back to their lines with a tight grip on their emotions and a stark reminder of their own mortality.

The high cost of their struggle was beginning to bear fruit, however. Three days after Fleetwood met the Great Emancipator, his home state abolished slavery during its constitutional convention. Maryland was also the home state of fellow black soldiers William H. Barnes, James H. Harris, and Alfred B. Hilton. It was the realization of a lifelong dream of Fleetwood's. What a difference a year made. Those who once walked in shackles now marched proudly in Federal blue. Fleetwood could remember the scouring eyes of slave masters searching for runaways among the ranks of black soldiers during drills in Baltimore a year earlier. Such servitude was now forever abolished. His cause was now shared by state as well as country. His prospects and those of his race seemed greater than ever. He was a battle-tested veteran. His goals in enlisting had been to help his race and further his own status. He had accomplished both.

Proof of Fleetwood's growing status came in the mail one clear, warm day. A letter from the Right Reverend Smith, bishop of Kentucky, extended an offer of a rectory in the Episcopal Church. The priesthood was tempting for Fleetwood. It offered the prestige and honor he sought. But he was beginning to feel what his commanders had already noticed. Some officers praised him as the most able enlisted man in the brigade. He had a natural inclination and aptitude for military life. He hoped to get a commission and forge a new direction for men of his race. Still, he agonized over the bishop's offer for ten days before responding. He wrote to Right Reverend Smith and Reverend Martin regretfully declining their generosity.

But the war still dragged on. Heady moments were interrupted by the jarring crash of cannon fire, a reminder that nothing had been settled. The war first had to be survived before one could enjoy the fruits of its labors. On Saturday, June 25, Fleetwood's regiment relieved the 6th and 22nd U.S. Colored Troops on the front, where fighting remained relatively quiet. He spent leisure time reading *Tom Cringle's Log*, a novel about life in the Royal Navy as a midshipman in the Caribbean, where war, piracy, smuggling, and slave running were rampant.

It was that very Saturday that Union forces embarked on a daring plan to end the Petersburg stalemate. The idea was simple, audacious, and seemingly brilliant: tunnel under the enemy's main barricade, plant massive explosives, and blow up the Confederates who were blocking access to the city.

The idea came from Union soldiers on the front line with extensive mining experience back home in Schuylkill County,

Pennsylvania. Their regimental leader, Colonel Henry Pleasants of the 48th Pennsylvania, peered at the imposing rebel battery one day desperately seeking some weakness to exploit. He heard one of his miner soldiers exclaim, "We could blow that damned fort out of existence if we could run a mine shaft under it."

What may have initially sounded like an outlandish idea gradually took hold. The suggestion levitated its way up the chain of command to Ambrose Burnside, where it might have died—except that Burnside had been an arms manufacturer before the war, and had experimented extensively with the use of gunpowder. He also had experience with civil mining operations. The knowledge that the men designing and digging the tunnel would be miners made the plan all the more feasible. He told Colonel Pleasants and his superior, General Robert Potter, that he would consider the plan. They came to his headquarters and discussed the details, after which Burnside ordered the work to begin. It could certainly do no harm to commence it, and it was probably better that the men should be occupied in that way, he thought.

When Burnside mentioned it to Meade, the commander of the Army of the Potomac was less than enthusiastic. Relations between the two men were strained and often competitive. Burnside had been the commander of the Army of the Potomac before Meade and outranked him, even if he was now Meade's subordinate. Meade said that he had no directions for siege operations at the front. That was for Grant to authorize. But he wouldn't order the work stopped. The two generals began to discuss the operation almost daily.

When the work on the mine began, many laughed and forecast failure. Some believed the tunnel would be too long, and men would not be able to breathe at its farthest extremes. Many watching suggested various methods to proceed. But Burnside trusted the experience of his miners and left the project in the hands of Colonel Pleasants and Colonel Potter.

A group of Federal engineers oversaw the digging of the tunnel. For the next month while the tunnel was being constructed, the black troops were stationed at the front where the rifle pits crossed the road leading from City Point to Petersburg. It was tedious and hazardous duty. Every day, someone from their ranks was either killed or wounded. They were so close to the enemy line that they didn't dare lift their heads above the breastworks for fear of drawing fire.

The weather grew unbearably hot, making life intolerable on the line. Fleetwood noted the oppressive heat as well as artillery fire in his June 26 diary entry. "Pretty hot with both balls and sun. Weather hot. Shells exploded throughout the day." He was hit with a spent shell on one occasion.

General Philip N. Sheridan's cavalry and wagon trains completed crossing the James River the same day to join the main army.

That Thursday, General Burnside's 9th Corps and 18th Corps made a charge on Petersburg and were driven back. The black troops listened to the assault but could not watch because of exploding shells. One man from Fleetwood's company was killed while on fatigue duty.

The days were monotonous. From behind their dirt and log fortifications, they watched a daily ritual of determined charges by both sides—the yelling of attacking troops followed by the staccato chorus of gunfire. The fortifications were too strong for either side to gain ground for very long.

On Friday, July 1, the rebels made a probing charge on the left side of the line of the black troops. The Union soldiers, crouched behind a line of rifle pits, responded with musket and artillery fire. The rebels sent a shower of lead screaming over their heads before being driven back. The black troops kept up the firing the rest of the day. One man from Fleetwood's regiment was wounded.

The black troops manned the trenches in shifts, three days on and two days in the rear. But days out were nearly as dangerous as those at the line. Their camp was close to the front and vulnerable to enemy shells. It was not uncommon for shrapnel to explode over tents and lodge in the earth.

For protection, the soldiers typically dug holes just long enough to lie down in and deep enough to sit up in. Poles covered the holes with two or three feet of earth to provide a shield against shrapnel. Fleetwood's hole became flooded on one damp, rainy day.

At the trenches, even going to the sinks was risky. Most men waited until night to relieve themselves. The sinks were placed in a wooded area, surrounded by small trees and saplings. Whenever a soldier ventured near them during daylight, the rebels would open fire. The trees bore hundreds of scars from the bullets.

The troops were relieved at nightfall. Each of the black regiments would leave the works together, filing out where the breastwork was high enough to offer protection and shield the flanks. One night, as the men prepared to leave, they came under enemy artillery fire. Confederate gunners from across the Appomattox had been able to spot them through field glasses and draw a bead on their position.

There were several close calls. On one occasion, black troops were about to march off when they heard the resounding boom of a cannon to their right, then the terrifying sound of a Whitworth shell speeding toward them. The specially bored, long-range British-made shell thundered past them along the entire length of the regiment, within six feet of their faces.

Some could even feel the hot air as the projectile whizzed by. It hit a mound of freshly upturned dirt about fifty feet from the end of their line and exploded. Amazingly, no one was hurt.

On another occasion, a Whitworth projectile actually struck Fielding Edwards of 6th U.S. Colored Troops, knocking him down but miraculously leaving him without serious injury. The men tried to take the constant danger in stride.

"We have an occasional casualty to relieve the monotony," Scroggs wrote dryly about the incident. "I suppose we might consider these Whitworth's tokens of love from our English Cousins. John Bull you're a brute."

As the soldiers gathered at camp, they talked about home. Some supposed the fields at home were being harvested. The wheat and rye were already ripe near Petersburg. But no one gathered the sheaves.

These were dark times for the country. The war-torn economy in the North was falling further into trouble. The price of gold had doubled since the first of the year to three hundred dollars an ounce, causing the dollar to lose 60 percent of its value. Shaking confidence further, Secretary of the Treasury Salmon P. Chase resigned.

Perhaps the only comfort was that life was even harder for the South. Deserters frequently crossed Union lines describing great deprivations. A week after Independence Day, one hundred North Carolinians gave up the cause.

The soldiers spent evenings telling tales or discussing the war. The feeling among the black troops was that they would again be left out of the heaviest fighting. There was even talk that they would be moved to another field of duty.

Not surprisingly, rumors abounded. There was talk of a big movement in the works from Grant. The word around camp was that the rebels were going to invade the North. General Jubal Early with forty thousand troops was being sent for the special duty. A few days later, they heard it was not Early but A. P. Hill. His men, it was said, had crossed the Potomac and were on a rampage through Maryland. Union general Lew Wallace was forced back to Baltimore, Fleetwood's hometown. Both the city and the capital were in danger.

For the soldiers poised to attack Petersburg, danger was a daily barrage of cannon and artillery fire. Even nightfall brought no relief from the pounding. Scroggs described the deadly music of the night: "There is never a minute night or day that the sound of firearms is not ringing in our ears. During the day the booming of heavy siege guns, the hurtling shells and screaming solid shot are continuous while the night is made hideous by the deep detonations of 13-inch mortars hurling their terrible missiles with fiery trains which bursts with an awful crash sufficient to almost awaken the dead. To all this the small arms of skirmishers and sharpshooters rattle a never ending accompaniment."

By the end of July, the men knew that something big was in the works. On July 22, Fleetwood noticed the 4th Division of Major General Ambrose Burnside's 9th Corps, U.S. Colored Troops, arriving at the front. It was a raw division. Leaders were being tight-lipped as the 9th's black troops began to drill daily for some special mission. Fleetwood and Kelly visited the men and saw several friends from Baltimore and talked of home. That same day, Sherman's southern lunge neared Atlanta.

The secret enterprise that the men suspected, but knew little of, was the tunnel. Work was progressing nicely.

The main tunnel was 522 feet long. It then split off into two side shafts at almost perpendicular angles for forty feet in each direction. Eight magazines branched from the side shafts like rooms from a hallway. The mine would be twenty-two feet below the enemy fort.

When it became clear that the tunnel could reach below the enemy battery, Burnside began to consider an assault to capitalize on the explosion. He wanted to use the raw recruits of the 9th Corps, General Edward Ferrero's 4th Division, which had not seen any action and had been stationed on army outposts. Part of his reasoning rested on the fact that many of his white troops were worn out. They had been fighting almost constantly since the siege began six weeks earlier. Not surprisingly, veteran troops often lost their zeal for attacking well-entrenched enemy lines. Sometimes when an order to advance came, men would charge a few feet, go to ground, fire a few shots, and then retreat.

Burnside thought that fresh troops might make a more vigorous charge, and directed General Ferrero to begin drilling his raw black troops for the operation. Burnside told Meade that he thought the chances were fair that a successful assault could be made from his front if it could be supported in specific way. The two men bickered over specifics, but Meade was under pressure from Grant to come up with a plan of attack. Meade told his boss that he did in fact have an operation in the works, Burnside's mine. No order for an attack was made, however. Meade was concerned that the position of the mine was less than ideal. Enemy guns and positions around the fort allowed the Confederates to sweep the field of any assault from three sides. Any such attack would have to be a complete surprise to the rebels and take advantage of the certain state of shock after the explosion.

Burnside and General Ferrero continued with details of the proposed assault while waiting for the go-ahead. Ferrero surveyed the terrain and created a plan to take Cemetery Hill, a crest about five hundred yards past the Confederate fort that overlooked Petersburg. Union leaders believed if the hill could be taken, Petersburg was theirs.

Ferrero's black troops drilled for the operation, practicing how they would charge around the crater that was anticipated from the explosion and sprint for the prize of Cemetery Hill. Despite their relative inexperience, the soldiers showed great promise, displaying an abundance of enthusiasm for the mission. The officers of these black regiments expressed great confidence in the ability of their men.

By then, the digging had been going on for a month. Burnside felt great pressure to spring the mine before all chance of a surprise was lost. He noticed reports in the Southern newspapers about rumors his men were digging a mine along the front. Union miners could also hear countermining near their own galleries. But heavy rain in recent days had likely filled the enemy tunnels and afforded the Union diggers a few more days.

Grant heard the same rumors, which by now had stretched beyond the bounds of reason. "We had learned through deserters who had come in that the people had very wild rumors about what was going on on our side. They said that we had undermined the whole of Petersburg; that they were resting upon a slumbering volcano and did not know at what moment they might expect an eruption."

One of the shafts nearly collapsed under the weight of the fort and the tremors from Confederate cannon fire above. The blue soldiers quickly braced the shaft, hoping it would hold and not bury them in a mass grave. On Wednesday, Burnside wrote Meade: "It is therefore probable that we escape discovery if the mine is to be used within two or three days. It is nevertheless highly important, in my opinion, that the mine should be exploded at the earliest possible moment consistent with the general interests of the campaign."

As the digging came to a completion, Meade and Burnside disagreed over how much explosive powder the mine should contain. Burnside wanted twelve thousand pounds, reasoning that a more potent explosion would create a hole with a greater radius and therefore lessen the incline on its sides. This would make it easier for troops to move forward after the explosion. Meade overruled, cutting the amount to eight thousand pounds.

But still no order to ignite the bomb came. Then events else-where triggered its need. Grant had General Hancock feign attack near Petersburg on Thursday, July 29. A large number of Confederate troops moved away from Burnside's position to block Hancock. So Grant ordered Burnside's men to take advantage of the opportunity and prepare for a Saturday attack.

Fleetwood, Veal, Hilton, Bronson, and the other black troops of the 2nd Division of the 18th Corps were ordered out of their trenches near the City Point road and marched to the area near the mine. They were to stand in reserve and support the charge by the 9th Corps black division. They lined up to the right of Burnside's men with orders to hold ground but not advance.

Burnside went to Meade's headquarters to discuss last-minute details. Like many of the Union brass, Meade showed a lack of faith in the fighting ability of black troops. "I cannot approve of your placing the Negro troops in the advance, as proposed in your project because I do not think they should be called upon to do as important a work as that which you pro-pose to do, certainly not called upon to lead," Burnside remem-bered him saying.

Burnside, who felt the attack stood a greater chance of suc-cess with fresh troops, didn't understand Meade's objection. He pointed out that the white troops had been under fire for the last six weeks. "These battle-torn veterans had, out of necessity and experience, developed the habit of protecting themselves from the fire. They were very much wearied, had contracted a habit of covering themselves by every method within their reach, and that I was satisfied they were not in a condition to make anything like as much of a dash upon the enemy's line as General Ferrero's division, which had not been under any considerable fire," he argued.

Meade responded that the mission could not hinge on a weak link. "[Burnside] should assault with his best troops," he said, "not that I had any intention to insinuate that the colored troops were inferior to his best troops, but that I understood that they had never been under fire; not that they should not be taken for such a critical operation as this, but that he should take such troops as from previous service could be depended upon as being perfectly reliable."

Burnside had another reason, which he left unexplained to Meade. He had seen the anxiety of many of the troops along the line as thousands of pounds of explosives were fed into the mine. Many feared for their own safety. He had consulted with his officers and all agreed that the explosion would not harm Union men, but convincing them was another matter. The general took comfort that the black troops, which had not yet been to the front, shared none of these concerns.

Meade said he would take up the issue of black troops with Grant. The next day, Meade and General Edward O. Ord, who was commanding the black regiments with Fleetwood, Veal, Hilton, and the others from the 18th Corps, conferred with Burnside and told him Grant ruled out using the black units in the advance of the movement. Grant's reasons were more political. "If we put the colored troops in front and [the assault] should prove a failure, it would then be said, and very properly, that we were shoving those people ahead to get killed because we did not care anything about them."

Burnside pleaded that the order be changed. "No, general, it cannot," he remembered Meade saying. "It is final." Meade sent a dispatch to Burnside to document Lieutenant General Grant's view: "I am instructed to say that the major-general commanding submitted to the lieutenant-general commanding the armies your proposition to form the leading columns of assault of the black troops, and that he, as well as the major-general commanding, does not approve the proposition, but directs that those columns be formed of the white troops."

By then it was Friday. The attack was just hours away with no time to drill other troops for the advance. In fact, it was an open question as to which troops would even lead the attack. Brigadier General Orlando Wilcox's men were closest to the position to make a charge. But these were among the most exhausted troops at the front. Brigadier General James H. Ledlie's troops were farther, but had less battle fatigue, and had proven their valor in battle.

"It will be fair to cast lots," Burnside decided. "Gen. Ledlie drew the winner or the lead at any rate. He immediately beamed with cheer, and quickly left to make the arrangements." The mine was scheduled to be ignited in just twelve hours, at 3:30 A.M.

The changes, however, created some problems. First, little thought was given to how the new arrangements might affect the troop movements of the assault. Ledlie's division was given no instructions to advance around the sides of the hole after the explosion and provide protection for the other troops. Burnside blamed Meade, saying, "The commanding general had been urgent in his views that in order to carry the crest that is, Cemetery Hill, that a dash must be made at it without reference to formation; that there would be no time for maneuvering."

Fleetwood and the black brigade of the 18th Corps, 2nd Division, were usually under Baldy Smith, were now temporarily in General Edward Ord's command. They spent the night changing positions as thousands of soldiers maneuvered into position and readied for the attack. The night was so pitch-black that Meade wondered if the troops could see those ahead of them. He messaged Burnside that the explosion could be postponed until visibility improved. But Burnside opted to proceed according to plan. Colonel Pleasants was ordered to strike the match and put the flame to the fuse.

In the minutes before the mine was scheduled to explode, thousands of troops squinted into the darkness for a view of the Confederate battery, waiting for the explosion like some gigantic starter's pistol that would unleash their sprint. Concerns of personal obliteration compounded the already highly anxious moments that await all soldiers before battle. Would they be swept away in a volcanic eruption of four tons of explosives, or possibly buried alive under mounds of earth? Of the effects of the blast, no one could be quite sure. If they survived the devices of their own commanders, they would then be tossed against the enemy defenses. There was considerable anxiety among the men before the explosion as to the effect that it might have upon them, Burnside noticed.

This anxiety only escalated in the slow, agonizing minutes before 3:30 A.M. The appointed time came, and passed in eerie silence. There was no explosion; the night remained still. The mine had been ready and charged for more than a week. Now it stalled. More minutes passed. The stress became almost unbearable. The delay seemed ominous.

Lieutenant James Scroggs of the 5th U.S. Colored Troops of

the 18th Corps with Beaty, Bronson, Pinn, and Holland expressed the feeling among the men. "The suspense became painful and strong hearts beat audibly and brave men trembled more from the fearful anxiety than a dread of the approaching conflict. . . . The moment of awful stillness preceding a battle, when brigades and divisions have silently filed into the places assigned them and then with baited breath await their orders to commence their sanguinary work, then it is that thought of home and dear ones that blanch the cheek and almost unnerve the bravest of the brave. The thought that before this sun shall set, our lifeless bodies may be trampled underfoot, our wife a widow and our children orphaned as if these moments were drawn out into hours, the armies would melt away for human nature could not stand it."

Burnside, waiting at a temporary headquarters at the 14th Battery near the center of the line, was beside himself. "Like every one else, [I] awaited with great anxiety the explosion of the mine," he said. "I need not say . . . that my anxiety on the occasion was extreme, particularly as I did not know the reason of the delay."

He waited for several minutes, wondering if there had been some miscalculation of the time for the fuse to burn. He sent an aide to find out what had happened. When word did not return shortly, he grew impatient and sent another. Meade felt a similar strain. And now Grant arrived at his headquarters to heighten the pressure. A telegraph line had been extended between his office and Burnside's, which he put to use.

The staccato tapping of the telegraph stroked Burnside's temper and furthered the resentment toward his boss. "Is there any difficulty in exploding the mine? It is three-quarters of an hour later than that fixed upon for exploding it," came Meade's electronic inquiry. Burnside didn't answer.

Thousands of troops waited, holding their breath and bracing for a thunderous quake. The tension was merciless.

Captain McMurray of the 6th U.S. Colored Troops with Thomas Hawkins and Alexander Kelly said, "I stood there until my eyes ached, and I could scarcely see. All was quiet, and we were in entire ignorance of what had occurred." Each minute seemed like an hour, and after an hour it seemed as if an eternity had passed.

Five minutes after Meade's first wire, he sent another. "Is General Burnside at his headquarters? The commanding general is anxious to learn what is the cause of delay."

Burnside again didn't answer. Finally, an exasperated Meade lost patience and ordered that if the mine had failed, Burnside must open artillery fire and order the charge against the undisturbed and still formidable enemy battery.

Burnside felt something must be done quickly. He was about to order the charge, when he decided to wait a bit longer. Perhaps he thought of the decimation of his troops at Fredericksburg twenty months earlier. "I will delay to ascertain what is the reason of the non-explosion of the mine," he decided.

He told one of Meade's aides that he had no idea why the trap had malfunctioned, and snapped that he'd let them know just as soon as he found out. Word finally came that a couple of brave soldiers from the regiment of Pennsylvania miners, Sergeant Harry Reese and Lieutenant Jacob Douty, volunteered for the unenviable task of crawling into the darkened tunnel, pushing past the dirt that had been placed to prevent a backfire from the shaft, to determine if the fuse had extinguished or was merely burning slowly. In the latter case, the mine could still explode and bury them alive. They found the fuse had detached at a splice about twenty-five yards into the tunnel. The men tied the ends together, relit the bomb, and scrambled out of the tunnel. General Potter reestimated the time for the explosion at 4:45 A.M., eleven minutes away.

Of course, this was more information than the thousands of apprehensive troops knew as they watched the first glint of sunlight emerge. Commanders tried to re-form the lines, which had become disordered as the flame from the fuse inched the final 475 feet to the point 22 feet beneath the enemy fort.

Then came the explosion, terrible to behold, lighting up the sky like an inferno. An eyewitness recalled the event: "A slight tremor of the earth for a second, then the rocking as of an earthquake, and with a tremendous blast, which rent the sleeping hills beyond, a vast column of earth and smoke shoots upward to a great height, its dark sides flashing out sparks of fire, hangs poised for a moment in mid-air, and then, hurtling down with roaring sound, showers of stones, broken timbers and blackened human limbs, subsides the gloomy pall of darkening smoke flushing to an angry crimson as it floats away to meet the morning sun."

From his view among the black troops, Scroggs was awestruck by the explosion. "The earth shook and quivered under our feet and with the smothered roar of an earthquake the mighty giant burst from confinement lifting the rebel fort with guns and garrison high in the air. Hardly had the reverberations ceased when another and more terrible roar burst with an awful cough from the iron throats of our hundred pieces of artillery. For one hour without cessation or interval the iron storm raged over our heads, the screaming hurtling missiles suggestive of ten thousand demons held high carnival in midair."

McMurray, standing with his men of the 6th U.S. Colored Troops with Hawkins and Kelly, happened to be looking directly at the rebel position when the mine exploded. "I first noticed the fort moving slowly, as if by a tremendous effort. Then all at once it seemed to leap up quickly to a height of perhaps a hundred and fifty feet, breaking into fragments of timber, stone, broken gun carriages, muskets, tents, and black and mutilated human bodies, all falling back quickly with a dull, sullen sound."

A total of 278 Confederates were killed by the explosion. Then the Union artillery began what Fleetwood described as fearful cannonading.

The shocked and horrified rebel troops who survived the blast scattered. The enemy works for about 150 to 250 yards on either side of the explosion were completely vacated. In place of the once impregnable battery lay a crater fifty to sixty yards long, twenty yards wide, and twenty-five feet deep.

The explosion had become so unsettling for the troops of Ledlie's division that it took five minutes for them to dust themselves off, gain their composure, and reestablish their lines. They scrambled over their own fortifications and channeled almost in single file through openings in a defensive line of sharpened wooden spikes. It was slow going in the early morning darkness. Footing was unstable in the loosened soil. The opened earth left the field strewn with mounds of dirt, debris, human body parts, and sections of fort.

The lines wavered and became broken as the men moved forward. Rather than forming a battle line, they moved in a column, which left them to advance unprotected a few men at a time. Worst of all, instead of avoiding the pit left by the blast, the confused men sought shelter in it and stopped.

These troops had seen too much enemy fire in recent weeks to make anything but a very cautious advance. One officer attributed the delay to "the breaking up of the column in consequence of the inequality of the ground and to the continual habit of the men for the last thirty or forty days of protecting themselves by almost every obstruction they came in contact with."

Their commanders yelled to urge them forward. One officer's hand became blistered from striking his men to induce them to make a dash for Cemetery Hill, a third of a mile past the crater. Soon the crater became a crowded convention of chaos with three utterly confused divisions.

"A total of 10,000 men—milling about, waiting in line as if at a train station, with hardly room to move side to side yet alone forward. The chasm did what the rebels could not do in the early minutes after the blast, stopping the Union advance and swallowing up thousands of men who in effect, disappeared," noted one observer.

The Union soldiers were, in fact, trapped. They were blocked from advancing by the sheer height of the walls of the crater, which at some points reached thirty feet. No ladders had been made available nor equipment to scale such obstacles. Troops in the rear couldn't advance because of the swarm of fellow troops ahead of them. Ledlie, the division commander of the assault troops, was safely awaiting the outcome in the bombproof safe area, even though it was his side that had ignited the bomb. When word came that his men wouldn't move forward, he sent an aide to inquire. He complained he couldn't go because of his malaria and that he had been hit by a spent shell. He swigged rum cajoled from a field surgeon to ease his discomfort.

Meade was handed a dispatch meant for Burnside in which an officer in the crater complained that the men would not move forward. "What is news from your assaulting column? Please report frequently," Meade telegraphed Burnside.

"We have the enemy's first line and occupy the breach. I shall endeavor to push forward to the crest as rapidly as possible," Burnside answered.

Thirty-five minutes passed and Ledlie's men had not advanced more than a couple hundred yards past the crater, a distance of less than half a mile from their starting point. Meade sent Burnside another message: "The commanding general learns that your troops are halting at the works where the mine exploded. He directs that all your troops be pushed forward to the crest at once."

The 18th Corps with the black regiments with Fleetwood, Beaty, Hawkins, and others were ordered to move forward past Ledlie's white division and take Cemetery Hill. They moved through a thousand-foot covered way that ran perpendicular to their lines. It was wide enough to accommodate troops moving in twos, and had been constructed to safely move men and supplies to the front. But when they came to the other end, they found it blocked with bottleneck congestion that prevented them from advancing.

Rebel prisoners captured in the minutes after the blast reported that there was no line behind the demolished fort and their men were retreating as the Union troops pushed forward. But crucial time was being lost amid the delays and confusion of the Federal troops. Meade saw the opportunity slipping away. He shot another message back to Burnside: "Our chance is now, push your men forward at all hazards (white and black), and don't lose time in making formations, but rush for the crest."

But Burnside was helpless, his assaulting columns were beyond his reach and his supporting lines were blocked from advancing. He was agitated by Meade's stream of wires. At 6:50 A.M., Meade questioned him again about the holdup. "What is the delay in your column moving? Every minute is most precious, as the enemy undoubtedly are concentrating to meet you on the crest, and if you gave them time enough you cannot expect to succeed. There is no object to be gained in occupying the enemy's line; it cannot be held under their artillery fire without much labor in turning it. The great point is to secure the crest at once, and at all hazards."

By then, two hours had passed since the surprise attack began with the demolition of the fort. The stunned rebels had since stopped running, had regrouped, and were mad as hornets with a fractured nest. They brought to bear every available cannon and rifle to the hollow of the hill the Union troops hoped to climb, and more rebel troops were on their way. For the first half an hour after the explosion, the fire had been quite light and the rebel cannonading ineffective. But shortly after, the delay to charge the hill became costly. The rebels rained down heavy fire from three sides. It was like shooting fish in the proverbial barrel.

Burnside telegraphed angrily in reply to Meade at 7:20 A.M. "I am doing all in my power to push the troops forward, and, if possible, we will carry the crest. It is hard work, but we hope to accomplish it. I am fully alive to the importance of it."

Meade shot back. "What do you mean by hard work to take the crest? I understand not a man has advanced beyond the enemy's line which you occupied immediately after exploding the mine. Do you mean to say your officers and men will not obey your orders to advance? If not, what is the obstacle? I wish to know the truth and desire an immediate answer."

Burnside lost his temper on receiving Meade's rebuke, and latched on to his demand for the truth. "I do not mean to say that my officers and men will not obey my orders to advance. I mean to say that it is very hard to advance to the crest. I have never in any report said anything different from what

I conceived to be the truth. Were it not insubordinate I would say that the latter remark of your note was unofficer-like and ungentlemanly."

By now, heavy enemy fire prevented an advance. A charge on the Union right side was quickly repulsed. Burnside had also thrown in the 4th Division of his 9th Corps, the black troops he had wanted to use to lead the assault. Instead of reacting like a supporting unit, they carried out their training as the leading assault force: they pushed past their white comrades in the crater and marched around the pit. They advanced about two hundred yards toward Cemetery Hill to an apple orchard. Many watching were impressed with their determination. "The colored division was put in, and from what I can learn no officers or men behaved with greater gallantry than they did," Burnside said.

They succeeded in capturing about two hundred Confederate soldiers and recaptured a stand of colors from a white regiment. But this caused them to pause for about half an hour at a critical moment. They stood unsupported in a precarious position. Just over the crest, Confederate troops had massed. The black troops lined up for a charge up the hill, but as they made their way they were soon exposed to furious enemy fire from all sides.

They fled in terror.

One officer described the wave of retreat as resembling a sand slide coming downhill. The black troops of Fleetwood's brigade were still behind their own lines, and watched the slaughter of their brethren unfold. In minutes, a third of the division was lost, 1,327 out of close to 4,000 that started out that morning.

Standing nearby, McMurray sympathized with the charging black soldiers. "During all this time I stood on our line of works, watching intently this life and death struggle. The only real fighting on our part was done by Burnside's black division. They fought desperately and determinedly, but before their charge was made the Confederates had two or three batteries in position, and had brought up a considerable force of infantry. The black men were forced back by a terrible artillery fire and a superior force of infantry. Never in all my experience did I see artillery do such awful execution as was done that morning in an apple orchard. It looked as if one side of hell had been opened, and fire and brimstone were belching forth. Finally the blacks were driven back and many of them took refuge in the crater. The white troops in the crater and just beyond were caught up in the flight. The enemy opened on them a destructive enfilading fire from all directions, solid shot, shell, grape and canister tearing through their ranks with terrible effect."

Scroggs, too, witnessed the onslaught. "From this slaughter pit they again advanced, but out of shape and much demoralized. The rebels met them with a withering fire, both of artillery and musketry, hewing passages through the already broken and confused lines. It was too much for human endurance and our men gave way. The rebs with a yell of triumph charged from their works, turned our right flank and captured near 1,200 prisoners."

General Butler was keeping an eye on the unfolding events. A member of his staff, B. C. Ludlow, sent frequent dispatches describing the scene. At 9:20 A.M., the news became dour. "The colored troops appear to have been massed, and charged over the breast-works, which appear to be held on one side by us, and the other side by the rebels. The colored troops were repulsed with considerable slaughter, and fled to the rear line of the breast-works; were rallied once; repulsed again, and again rallied to be repulsed. From my position I see them trying to rally them without avail."

The morning's opportunity for victory had vanished, replaced with a Confederate rout. By 9:30 A.M., Grant and Meade thought it judicious to cancel the assault and order a withdrawal. The crater of the mine was so overcrowded with men that it would be nothing but murder to send any more men forward there, Meade said.

Men, however, were still trapped in the crater. Evacuating it exposed them to enemy fire. Some tried to run out and back to the Union entrenchment, only to be shot down. A mass of bodies was scattered between the chasm and the Federal line.

"You can exercise your discretion in withdrawing your troops now or at a later period, say tonight," Meade told Burnside. "It is not intended to hold the enemy's line which you now occupy any longer than is required to."

Burnside wanted to fight on. But none of his divisional commanders agreed. Neither did Grant.

The troops remained hostages of the crater throughout most of the day. At 2 P.M., just as they were ready to fall back, the rebels stormed the pit and drove them back to the Federal line with heavy casualties.

The defeat was bitter. Many of the troops blamed the Union high command. "It was with sorrow and chagrin we beheld this disaster knowing as we did that there was no excuse for it. . . . Someone high in command has been criminally negligent and I hope will receive the punishment which such conduct so richly merits," Scroggs wrote in his diary that day. "By just such villainous carelessness about details, this bloody and ruinous war has been unnecessarily prolonged." He found that ten men from the regiment of Beaty, Bronson, Pinn, and Holland, the 5th U.S. Colored Infantry, were wounded or killed.

Brigadier General Edward Ferrero complained that his division of black troops was needlessly slaughtered. He believed that his men should have led the assault. "I am forced to believe that the Fourth Division (colored division) would have made a more impetuous and successful assault than the leading division. I have not the slightest doubt from the manner in which they went in, under very heavy fire, that had they gone in in the first instance, when the fire was comparatively light, but that they would have carried the crest of Cemetery Hill beyond a doubt."

Cries rose up for an inquiry into the debacle from the lower ranks to the high command. President Lincoln ordered such. Burnside, who lost 3,838 men during the battle, was relieved of command. Ledlie was dismissed from the service. Several other commanders were cited for poor planning and lack of battlefield leadership.

But across the country, the news of the disaster that would become known as the Crater fiasco caused tongues to wag. People who didn't see the withering fire the black troops had endured now only heard and talked of their flight in terror. The worst fears about black soldiers had been confirmed. For Fleetwood and the other black soldiers in Hinks's division, this was a bitter pill. The respect their heroics in June had gained for black soldiers suddenly was lost.

They had fought for nearly a year now, but as summer closed their labors and bitter sacrifices had been for a season without a harvest.

⊷

TEN

THE PRICE OF HONOR
Heroics at New Market Heights

In enlisting in the Union army, Fleetwood and other black troops knew they ran the risk of being tortured and hanged if captured by the Confederates. But by mid-September 1864 the rebels had devised a harsh new punishment for captured black soldiers. They made them slaves.

Among the newly enslaved captives were men who served with Fleetwood, Veal, and Holland. Like Fleetwood, many of these soldiers had never been slaves and withered under the loss of their freedom.

Colonel Samuel Duncan, who commanded the 4th, 6th, and 22nd U.S. Colored Troops, realized how potentially demoralizing the new threat could be to his troops. The best way to abruptly end this abominable Confederate practice, he believed, was to threaten rebels with similar treatment. He sent a message to Butler seeking permission to use rebel prisoners as slave labor to build Union fortifications. Duncan relished the prospect of his men, who included former slaves, guarding former slave masters.

"It is now established with sufficient certainty that the rebels have remitted to slavery, or otherwise put to hard labor, colored prisoners of war captured from us at Plymouth, Petersburg, and elsewhere, to warrant the use of rebel prisoners upon the work now in progress at Dutch Gap, where the shells of the enemy are beginning to tell with considerable effect upon our laboring soldiers. My men would take pleasure in acting as guards; would perform the duty, I think, with unusual pride and efficiency."

Union leaders, however, had other plans for his men. Butler, in particular, wanted to remove the cloud of doubt over black troops since the Crater fiasco. Lieutenant General Grant blamed the failure on Union generals. But the disaster resurrected doubts throughout the North about the fighting ability of black troops. This suspicion was especially bitter for the black troops in the Army of the James. Many complained that they had been put through some of the hardest duty and labor of the war but had been given few opportunities for battle.

Butler saw an opportunity to prove the value of his black soldiers. His focus turned to a coveted piece of ground outside of Richmond called New Market Heights. He told Grant that the black troops had been particularly effective in storming the works outside Petersburg in June and were unusually motivated in battle.

The black troops at the head of the attack at the crater were inexperienced and badly led, Butler pointed out. But regiments under Colonel Draper and Colonel Duncan were hardened and battle-tested. Butler's intelligence reported that despite the importance of the Southern capital, the Confederates had left the city thinly protected. About thirty-five hundred soldiers held a line almost ten miles long. Butler could lead a force of twenty-three thousand men against the enemy. Most of Lee's army was stationed defending the railroads and vital supply lines around

Petersburg or with Early, who was battling Sheridan in the Shenandoah Valley. Grant wanted to prevent Lee from sending troops to Early, which might turn the tide against Sheridan. Butler proposed an attack to capture Richmond. Grant thought such an advance would, at the very least, prevent reinforcements against Sheridan.

Even a thin line of troops, however, held advantages against a superior force because of the extensive fortifications outside Richmond. Butler wanted to attack a hill near the New Market Road where twice before white Union troops had been beaten back with heavy losses. He astutely reasoned that black troops, hungry as they were for battle glory and wary against capture or defeat, might prevail where white troops had failed. The recollection of his black troops outside Petersburg was fresh in his mind.

He suggested that many of those same black troops under Colonel Duncan and Colonel Draper take the lead in the upcoming siege. "I want to convince myself whether the Negro troops will fight, and whether I can take, with the Negroes, a redoubt that turned [Major General Winfield S.] Hancock's corps on a former occasion."

Grant approved the plan and sent Butler a message on the morning of September 27 to "make all your changes of troops at once, ready for the execution of orders verbally communicated, so as to have troops as fresh as possible." Thousands of troops, including the black infantry regiments along with cavalry units and artillery, began to mobilize along the James.

Grant wanted the attack made at night. Troops, led by the black regiments, would cross the James River over pontoon bridges and attack the enemy lines across from Deep Bottom and Aiken's House. Two columns would move in unison and within reach of each other. The charge would begin at dawn. Once the earthworks defenses were broken, the remaining troops would pour beyond the Confederate lines and march to the city. Cavalry units would follow the foot soldiers over the works and race toward Richmond.

A swift attack was critical. Grant wanted to prevent the rebels from diverting troops from Petersburg, which lay south, to the north side of the river. "The object of this mission is to surprise and capture Richmond," the lieutenant general ordered.

He suggested that the invading Union forces follow roads as near the river as possible. The Confederates were entrenched on the north side of the bank of the James across from Deep Bottom with Richmond to their backs. A garrison was entrenched at Chaffin's Farm. If the Union forces could capture these troops, Grant wanted them held only in passing. Richmond was the prize, not prisoners. If the enemy fortifications could not be taken, then the Federals were ordered to dig trenches and pin the rebels down with a light force and proceed to the city.

Grant ordered the soldiers to travel light. Union men would only be allowed to take a single blanket roll, three days' rations in haversacks, and sixty rounds of ammunition. No wagons would be taken.

A simultaneous invasion would be launched against Petersburg. Grant believed that the rebels would be forced to leave one of the cities open to attack in order to protect the other. He ended his orders saying, "The prize sought is either Richmond or Petersburg, or a position which will secure the fall of them later."

The same day, Tuesday, September 27, Fleetwood spent the hours attending his usual errands. After writing out reports, he crossed the river with Hawkins. They visited friends at the 22nd U.S. Colored Troops, which regiment was now also serving in Colonel Draper's brigade. Fleetwood retired at 10 P.M., but his regiment was awakened and called out for duty. Fleetwood was surprised and noted that the regiment got out "after much tribulation and several unsuccessful attempts to catch a nap."

At 1:15 A.M., Major General Butler sent a message to Major General David Bell Birney, asking why he had not started moving his troops yet. Birney responded that he understood that the movement would begin the next day. "You had better move tonight as to have your troops fresh tomorrow to prepare for embarkation," Butler responded at 1:45 A.M.

Birney messaged back that it was too late to move the men that night. "I will, with your permission, not start until tomorrow evening, and will promise to not delay the boats at all. My preparations are all made for that time."

The next day, they left Dutch Gap and the lines outside of Petersburg around 3 P.M. and headed in the direction of Richmond, embarking on a gunboat for transport to Jones' Landing. They made a quick camp at Deep Bottom, a point along the James about twelve miles south of Richmond. Thousands of troops congregated in anticipation of the attack.

Butler had passed along Grant's battle orders to his army along with more detailed instructions of his own. He planned to use every available force that could be spared from his army for the siege of Richmond and the defense of posts along the river.

He ordered a floating bridge installed by midnight September 28. It was covered with manure and straw to muffle the thunderous noise of crossing troops that might alert the rebels at Aiken's Landing. The 18th Corps, with the exception of the black division, under Ord would cross the river at that point and head north toward Richmond as the first column. Another column, led by Birney and which would include the black troops and General August Valentine Kautz's cavalry, would cross another floating bridge at Deep Bottom. The black division would take the point of attack against the rebel fortifications on the high ground called New Market Heights. Once they gained the works, Kautz's cavalry would be able to spring into action and race toward Richmond.

Butler estimated that the rebels held a line of earthworks extending for several miles along the north side of the river from Signal Hill, past Aiken's House, and to New Market and beyond. Most of the fortifications consisted of carefully constructed abatises, felled trees with limbs and trunks sharpened to deadly edges and set in the ground at dangerous angles to slow cavalry and foot soldiers. His information told him that the Confederate troops holding the gray line included Bushrod Johnson's 450-man Tennessee brigade, which had advance guards extending toward Dutch Gap. Johnson's men held about thee-quarters of a mile of ground. The 25th Virginia with about 200 men was opposite Deep Bottom, along with Colonel Dudley M. Du Bose's 400 men from a Georgia brigade.

The works at New Market Heights, which Butler planned to attack with black troops, was strongly fortified and held by John Gregg's Texas brigade of 400 men. The only other Confederate infantry force was a militia reserve with about 175 men, camped at a considerable distance in the rear. The unit was made up of soldiers either younger than eighteen or older than forty-five, most of whom, Butler surmised, had never been under fire.

Other regiments were scattered in the area. But Butler's force had vastly superior numbers, boosting his confidence. "It will be seen, therefore, that these bodies of which we have knowledge, if the information is correct, should be 2,875 men, and it may be safely predicted that there are not 3,000 effective men outside of the limits of the city of Richmond on the north side of the river. It is upon this information, which is fully credited, that the movement is largely based."

The thinly stretched gray troops of less than thirty-five hundred men between the Appomattox and the James defended a line of almost ten miles. The nearest body of possible reinforcements was eleven miles south, near Petersburg.

Butler echoed Grant's reminder that the attack depended on a quick strike, coordinated with joint movement from the two advancing Federal columns. He directed Major General Ord to move a division under the cover of night to the north side of the river near the Varina Road. Just before daybreak at 4:30 A.M., the blue troops would launch an attack at the enemy line. Rebel gunboats along the river two miles away could only provide an "annoyance," Butler said. If Ord's drive was successful, his objectives were to try to capture Fort Harrison, storm the enemy line from behind, and destroy Confederate bridges to prevent a counterattack. Ord was also directed to send troops up the Osborne Turnpike and head for Richmond.

Ord's thrust would occur simultaneously with a charge led by General Birney, whose fifteen thousand troops, including the black divisions of about twenty-five hundred men temporarily assigned to him, would move out from Deep Bottom and attempt to break the formidable works at New Market Heights.

Both columns would join forces near Richmond. Perhaps thinking of the delays that proved costly near Petersburg in May and June, Butler stressed the need for speed and precision. "If the movement is made with celerity; if the march is held uninterruptedly as much as possible, and if in the first attack the element of unity of time is observed, which has been greatly neglected in some of the movements of the army, we shall gain over the enemy, so far as any considerable re-enforcements are concerned, some eight to twelve hours, and perhaps more of valuable time, which ought not to be lost, and which should bring us far on our journey in the twelve miles which we are to go."

The rebel force defending Richmond was small enough, Butler believed, that Federal troops could move quickly toward the city before reinforcements could arrive. At the earliest, troops could not be diverted for at least six hours and such movements would leave the vital Confederate lines abandoned. That would allow the Union army to send in as many reinforcements as the South. And once the two columns were joined, the blue force would exceed twenty-three thousand men.

Butler promised to recommend for promotion every soldier from the first regiments to enter Richmond—from the colonels leading brigades down to the privates. They would also receive six months' extra pay.

To ensure secrecy, the men were not told the details of the mission until just hours before the attack. Thousands of Federal troops left Petersburg on Wednesday and made the twelve-mile march to the James. Engineers began building the floating bridge—comprised of small boats lashed together—at 7:30 P.M. to prevent early detection by the rebels. The low tide was uncooperative and added three hours to the construction. The last nine boats for the bridge had to be dragged over the soft mud and positioned by hand. The work was finished at 2 A.M., just an hour before the troops were scheduled to cross. It spanned 1,320 feet and required sixty-seven boats and two for the draw.

Because of Birney's miscommunication over the timetable to move his troops, many of the black troops reached Deep Bottom fatigued and sleepy, just hours prior to the launching of the attack. Their steamer pushed off at sunset and arrived at Deep Bottom at midnight. The men tried to sleep in the open air until being roused for the attack shortly before 3 A.M. They saw thousands of soldiers milling around quietly in the darkness on the south side of the James. They drank coffee and talked quietly about the mission before them.

Despite their superior numbers, the black troops faced some serious obstacles in spearheading the attack. Because the movement had to be made quickly, they couldn't afford to wait for artillery units to cross the river and soften the Confederate defenses. Butler reasoned that if the attack became a cannon duel, it was doomed to failure. The general also ordered the men to refrain from shooting at the enemy as their lines advanced. He believed it would slow their movement and possibly endanger soldiers ahead of them.

Many of the men, fully aware of the danger they faced, carefully wrote out their name, hometown, and regiment in legible letters on notes pinned to their clothes. These forerunners of dog tags would help identify their bodies for notification of loved ones should their corpses become badly mangled or disfigured in battle.

Captain McMurray, like thousands of other soldiers, didn't fully realize what lay before him. "Had I known when I arose that morning what was in store for my company, for my regiment, within the next two or three hours, I would have been entirely unfitted for the duties of the day."

The black troops crossed at Deep Bottom while Ord's column crossed upstream at Aiken's Landing. As they began to cross the river, the manure-covered planks failed to deaden the sound sufficiently to avoid enemy notice. The dulled thuds of thousands of marching feet alerted the rebels to the troops' movements. But the attack had been such a carefully guarded secret that this was the Confederates' first warning.

At 4:15 A.M., just fifteen minutes before the first light of dawn, Butler rode out to address the three thousand black troops gathered on a plain that shelved toward the river. He pointed toward the enemy fortifications and told the men they would have to take it by bayonet charge. "Those works must be taken by the weight of your column; not a shot must be fired." The men were ordered to remove the percussive caps from the locks of their rifles to prevent accidental firing.

To stiffen their resolve, he reminded them, none too subtly, that they could not afford to fail or be captured, that such fates were worse than death. He coaxed their fighting fire by reminding them of the senseless slaughter of black troops at Fort Pillow by Confederate forces led by Nathan Bedford Forrest in April. And he urged that when they clamored over the rebel defenses to face the enemy in hand-to-hand combat their battle cry be: "Remember Fort Pillow."

As the first light broke through the thinning morning fog, the men began to move out toward the rebel fortifications. Draper's brigade was in the center at the point of attack. This included the black regiments of the 5th with Beaty, Bronson, Pinn, and Holland; the 36th with Gardiner and James; and the 38th with Barnes, Harris, and Ratcliff. To the immediate left marched Duncan's black troops that included the 4th Regiment with Fleetwood, Veal, and Hilton and the 6th with Hawkins and Kelly.

They crossed through a wooded area and emerged into an open field on the crest of a hill. The first ray of sunlight appeared over the tops of trees beyond the field. The morning air was dank and foggy. Through the mist, they could see the daunting task before them. The troops would have to cross a stretch of Four-Mile Creek from the enemy works and then fight their way through thick underbrush that was divided by a leg of the creek and swampy marshland—all while well within range of the defending rifles. Beyond that, the Southerners had piled the trunks of trees, sharpened sticks, and fence posts to entangle an oncoming force. About 150 yards in front of the enemy, trees had been leveled and branches and limbs sharpened as an abatis to force soldiers to stop as rebels took aim. About fifty yards beyond that, sharpened stakes had been erected to prevent cavalry advances.

The other obstacle was perhaps the most deadly. The woody debris would channel the advancing black troops through a few narrow openings. At some points the opening was just a few yards. The Confederates could concentrate their fire on those points and level the soldiers as if firing in a shooting gallery.

The troops moved forward, a sea of twenty-five hundred black soldiers, over the uneven turf in the misty dawn. Many sequestered fears of impending destruction. Thoughts of the cruel massacre of black soldiers at Fort Pillow stirred their emotions and fueled their anxieties. They looked out over the imposing fortifications, the long grassy plain on which they would be exposed to enemy fire, the swamp and creek, the debris and sharpened stakes meant to ensnare them at the most dangerous points of the charge. They would have no choice but to press on into the face of the torrent. Retreat offered no solace. Capture would mean the shackles of slavery or death, most likely at the end of a rope like a common criminal. Flight would mean disgrace to their race, their family and friends, and would set back their claims for liberty, equality, and respect. They needed to prove their valor and answer the questions, no matter what the cost, even unto death.

They knew as they crept closer to the enemy that their mission was almost suicidal. Other troops had stormed these very positions and twice failed. Perhaps their commanders felt their lives expendable. The enemy lay in wait up ahead, protected behind barriers, honing their sights at that very moment. They prayed they could advance faster than the rebels could load and reload. Without question, many of them would feel the ravishing blows of enemy fire and not live out the day. Still, on they marched.

Skirmishers were sent in advance of the marching columns, searching through the tall late-summer grass for the glint of Southern rifles and bayonets. Within twenty minutes of the start of the march, the crisp sound of shots echoed in the air as black troops in Duncan's brigade discovered rebel pickets at the edge of a woody ravine along Four-Mile Creek.

The gunfire, a sharp, staccato drumroll of punctuated discharges, signaled the Union advance and made hearts beat faster. The rebel pickets bolted for their defensive lines and some of the black troops gave chase, sending the enemy scurrying over the long open field in front of their earthworks. The rebels occasionally turned to return fire at the pursuing black soldiers, some of whom came as close as the abatis. The Southerners, scrambling over the parapet, were just yards away.

Behind the log-and-earth fortifications, the rest of the Confederates lowered their sights on the oncoming black Federal soldiers. Behind the wall lay two thousand gray-clad soldiers, including sharpshooters from the 1st, 4th, and 5th Texas from Brigadier General John Bell Hood's Texas Brigade, the 24th Virginia Cavalry, and the Rockbridge Artillery.

The black troops marched across the open field to the edge of the fallen timber obstacles and formed in line with as much care and precision as if on parade. The captains stood at the front of the ranks of each company, with first sergeants in the rear rank. The lieutenants and the sergeants stood a step or two behind the rear ranks, and a few paces behind them stood the field officers of each regiment, followed by the brigade and staff officers.

As the lines positioned, the Confederates waited patiently without firing a single shot. "I have no doubt but they looked on with great interest, thinking no doubt, what a lot of fools we were," McMurray thought.

The eerie silence heightened the tension to an almost unbearable pitch. The prospect of death was certain. McMurray described the apprehension as the men faced their own mortality. "I know there was a big lot of thinking done by us while we stood there. We knew there was a strong line of Confederates behind the rifle pits, across the slashing from us. We knew that as soon as we would move forward they would open fire on us. We knew the order to go forward would soon be given. But beyond that what? Would it be death or capture? Would it be victory or defeat? How the scenes and deeds of the past came rushing in on the mind like a mighty flood! That was perhaps the most trying five minutes or ten minutes we endured in all our army life. It would require the pen of the mightiest angel that ever stood before the throne of God to write down the thoughts of the men who stood in that line that bright September morning."

About 5:30 A.M., with the fog clearing, Butler ordered the black soldiers to shoulder their arms and advance. Colonel Duncan cried, "Forward." As a single body, the black troops moved toward the enemy. Not a man from the regiment turned back.

As the command to move was given, Lieutenant John B. Johnson of Company B swung his sword over his head in circles. After just a few revolutions, an enemy bullet struck his wrist. The sword flew twenty feet and landed on the ground.

The 683 black troops under Duncan, which included Fleetwood, Hilton, Veal, Hawkins, and Kelly, jutted out in front of the rest of the force. The other regiments stopped to wait for further orders and for the slow-arriving reinforcements.

The black soldiers yelled as they advanced. A thunderous storm of fire exploded from the behind the enemy earthworks. The ground shook as if an earthquake had been unleashed. The

Union lines became splintered and fragmented as dozens of soldiers fell. The screams of the wounded amplified the anguish.

Pioneer cutters rushed to the brush to cut an opening for the troops. The rebels concentrated their fire on them. Within seconds, their ranks were mowed down. Men fell over their cutters into the undergrowth. Other black troops rushed to grab their axes and began to hack at the abatis. They too fell.

Duncan, whose brigade had been the first to charge, was hit four times and fell severely wounded. Within minutes, hundreds of bodies lay strewn over the battlefield, which was now soaked in blood. In the confusion, it became almost impossible for the men to get their bearings. Smoke from the enemy guns filled the air, and the orderly ranks scattered. The noise from the gun and artillery fire was so loud that men could scarcely hear.

The charge was on the verge of a disastrous collapse, especially after many of the regimental and company commanders were annihilated. The black troops were left in the open field under galling rebel fire without leaders to guide them forward or back to safe harbor. A massacre was unfolding. With every agonizing second, more black troops fell.

"It was sheer madness," Fleetwood thought as they advanced in the withering fire with guns rendered useless except for hand-to-hand combat.

The slaughter was unmerciful.

"It was slow work, and every step in our advance exposed us to the murderous fire of the enemy," McMurray noted. "As we urged our way onward, we were utterly unable to protect ourselves in any way. As we advanced I noticed our ranks getting thinner and thinner, and wondered what was becoming of my men. . . . We had no possible chance for success, and the enemy had full opportunity to butcher us at will. It was a wonder that as many of us escaped as did. It was only because the firing on both sides made such a dense smoke that the Johnnies could not see to take aim, that we escaped as well as we did."

Captain Samuel Vannuys, the young officer from Indiana who had reluctantly joined the black troops, was shot and killed. Emmanuel Patterson, who had been ill that morning but ordered by the doctor to duty, was hit in the abdomen, his flesh ripped open. His bowels fell from his body, and he caught them up with his hand. First Sergeant Miles Parker was shot through the leg. He fell to the ground but yelled to his captain, "Never mind 'em, Captain, I'll get along all right."

Hundreds fell in the charge, including Jeremiah Walker, William Lucas, Richard Bryant, Nathaniel Danks, Charles Gibson, Charles Hubarb, Noah Jones, Charles Johnson, Samuel Johnson, William Kenney, and Thomas Keyser.

Fleetwood, caught in the crossfire, thought he would surely die. A bullet passed between his legs. It sliced his bootstrap, trousers, and stockings but left his skin unscathed. A bullet passed so close to Corporal Charles Veal that it scratched his skin. "It was a deadly hailstorm of bullets sweeping men down as hail-stones sweep the leaves from trees," Fleetwood moaned.

As sergeant major, he led the left side of his regiment. A sergeant standing near him carried the colors. A bullet cut through the flag staff, severing it in two, before striking his body. The man stood momentarily still holding the broken staff before falling to the ground. Alfred B. Hilton, the powerfully built Maryland farmer, immediately grabbed hold of the flag and took the place of the fallen sergeant. But within seconds, he too was struck by a bullet in the leg. He lifted the flag high as he fell to the ground, yelling urgently amid the chaos, "Boys, save the Colors."

The rebels concentrated their fire on the color bearers. Fleetwood and Veal watched two soldiers fall protecting the

Union colors. They rushed instantly to take up the hazardous duty, answering Hilton's plea, racing over to grab the colors before they touched the Virginia earth. Fleetwood grabbed the American flag and Veal saved the blue flag. The banners had been presented to the black regiment by the ladies of Baltimore before they left home almost exactly a year earlier.

Fleetwood knew the importance of saving the flag.

Preserving the colors was more than just a symbolic act of chivalry. Keeping the regimental flag and Old Glory lifted skyward was critical for a regiment's survival in the fog of battle, where smoke and enemy fire could be disorienting.

The flag helped soldiers maintain their position and bearings as men fell around them and the battlefield became veiled in smoke. The colors kept the vital line of communications open with the rest of the army. Couriers between commanders and regiments needed the flags to spot the men in the field. When the colors fell, the spirit of the regiment often went with them. Soldiers became lost in the confusion. Battle ranks fell apart, and the link with the rest of the army vanished.

Thus the color guard was a prime target for enemy fire. Even as he hoisted the regimental flag skyward with a rallying cry to his fellow troops, Fleetwood had no doubt that enemy snipers were training their sights on him. But if he died today, he wanted to be remembered as the man who saved the colors.

In the dim early light, amid the fog and the intense smoke from enemy fire, the charge seemed lost in the chaos. No commissioned officer was in sight. Then suddenly, there were Fleetwood and Veal waving the near-sacred colors and rallying eighty-five survivors of their regiment to make another final charge at the enemy works. Enemy shells exploded around them and Confederate soldiers fired on them from both flanks. Some men made it past those obstacles, only to feel the brunt of the enemy's fury.

Alexander Kelly, a sergeant in the 6th, had advanced just short of the line of abatis and debris when his color guard was wounded. There, amid the confusion and in "a place of the greatest possible danger," he seized the fallen colors and raised them, rallying his men. Sergeant Major Thomas R. Hawkins also saved his regimental colors and spurred the men forward.

The gunfire was so intense that Fleetwood and others retreated to the abatis. Fleetwood and Veal scrambled back to their line after enduring half an hour's exposure to rebel fire. They had saved the colors and pulled their men together. But the hill had not been taken.

Of the twelve color bearers who began the charge only one walked from the field. Of the 683 black soldiers who began the attack, 365—more than half—were killed or wounded.

General Butler watched the charge unfold from the first hill near the Heights. "The column marched down the declivity as steadily as possible. At once when it came in sight the enemy opened upon it," he said. "The enemy concentrated their fire upon the head of the column, which looked at one moment as if it would melt away. The colors of the first battalion went down, but instantly they were up again, but with new color-bearers."

It became apparent to Fleetwood and the others that the task of taking the rebel works was too much for the two regiments of black troops, the 4th and 6th. "Strong earthworks, protected in front by two lines of abatis, and one line of palisades, and in the rear by a lot of men who evidently knew how to shoot, and largely outnumbered us," was his cold assessment.

As the black soldiers fell back, the Confederates jumped over the parapet and began to strip the bodies of the dead and wounded. Vannuys, who didn't want to leave the army a mere private, lay in the field a dead captain. A rebel soldier took his watch, money, and clothes.

Southerners scooped up rifles and anything else of value. The shoes were taken from the dead men's feet and pockets were turned inside out, cartridge boxes and haversacks were taken.

But within twenty minutes, the Union lines were re-formed and orders for another charge were given.

Draper's brigade of the 5th, 36th, and 38th U.S. Colored Troops followed Duncan's in support. These regiments included Beaty, Bronson, Pinn, and Holland along with Gardiner, James, Barnes, Harris, and Ratcliff. They marched past Chaffin's Farm over an open field. Rebel skirmishers opened fire from the woods. The troops descended into a ravine and lay on the ground.

Brigadier General Charles Paine, overlooking the scene, sent an order to Draper to move his brigade to the right where the troops were getting the worst of it. Draper's troops formed lines farther down the ravine, but were still exposed to the fire of rebel batteries from New Market Heights, although the guns had little effect. They lay in the moist morning grass for about half an hour. At 8 A.M., Draper was ordered to form his brigade and make another assault on the enemy's works.

It was a directive that left a sinking feeling in the most courageous heart. Before them lay a scene of carnage. Hundreds of their comrades lay dead or writhing in pain on the battlefield. The fallen were now obstacles in their path. They would be exposed to the same thunderous fire that had leveled those men just minutes before. Any cover from the morning fog had disappeared as the sun illuminated the battlefield.

But the commanders made one significant change in the attack. The black soldiers were allowed to place their percussive caps in their rifles and shoot at the enemy as they advanced.

The lines readied for the charge. And the same trepidation

that ran through the ranks of black soldiers of Draper's brigade now ran through Duncan's men. Some lost heart. Lieutenant Samuel S. Simmons (whose real name was later discovered to be De Forest), a white officer of the 36th and acting aide-de-camp of Draper, abandoned his post at the ravine and headed back to the safety of Deep Bottom without bothering to notify his superior. But the black troops pressed forward.

The 22nd U.S. Colored Troops opened the charge with a skirmish on the left of Draper's brigade, but did not advance to the works. Draper's black troops passed through three hundred yards of young pine trees and then marched over the open field of more than eight hundred yards toward the rebel fortifications.

The shout to "charge" went up and the men rushed forward, yelling loudly in a ferocious chorus meant to intimidate the enemy. An explosion of rebel fire erupted and hundreds of troops stumbled and fell. The piercing screams of the wounded were as frightening as the exploding guns. Ranks were decimated as men fell on the bodies of the slain and wounded from Duncan's brigade. Those left standing turned toward the fury and braced themselves as if shielding from a rainstorm. They came within twenty yards of the Confederate line when they were forced to cross a swamp and wade through a shallow stream, breaking their lines. They re-formed on the bank within earshot of the rebels.

"At this juncture, too, the men generally commenced firing, which made so much confusion that it was impossible to make the orders understood," Draper noted. "Our men were falling by scores. All the officers were striving constantly to get the men forward. I passed frequently from the right to the left, urging every regimental commander to rally his men around the colors and charge."

Several of the white officers, such as Lieutenant Colonel Shurtleff and Captains Fashion, Cock, and Marvin, fell severely wounded. Some of the men became discouraged in the confusion, but others rushed headlong into enemy fire. Several black companies were left without officers.

The charge threatened to disintegrate into a hopeless slaughter. Any semblance of order had disappeared. With the attack faltering, and the lives of hundreds of men at stake, black enlisted men rallied the troops under galling fire. Despite an overwhelming temptation to retreat, the fortitude and resolve that Butler remembered from the Petersburg siege and now counted on emerged within the splintered ranks. Enlisted black troops rose up to lead their men forward. In the midst of the storm, they began to yell a clarion call for valor. The troops began to answer, first one soldier and then another. A chorus began as more men began to yell back. A whooping holler went up that seemed to infuse courage in their veins.

"After half an hour of terrible suspense, by starting the yell among a few, we succeeded in getting them in motion," Draper noted. "The entire brigade took up the shout and went over the rebel works."

Butler would remember the battle cry for years. "With a cheer and a yell which I can almost hear now, they dashed upon the fort. But before they reached even the ditch, which was not a formidable thing, the enemy ran away and did not stop until they had run four miles."

Milton Holland, the former slave who once ended a letter home with the rallying cry "Give me liberty or give me death," called out to rally Company C of the 5th and directed a charge to the enemy line. James H. Bronson took command of his company. Robert Pinn was shot and wounded, but ignored his injury and led Company I in the advance. Powhatan Beaty, the simple farmer from Cincinnati, took command of Company G and directed them forward.

The Confederates were stunned to see the black troops continuing to advance despite their fire. Miles James had come within thirty yards of the rebel fortifications when he was struck by an enemy bullet that shattered his arm, badly mutilating it and putting it in need of immediate amputation. In great pain, with blood streaming from his wounds, he loaded his weapon, then raised his one useful hand and urged his men forward.

Many rebels began to retreat from the works as the Union troops drew closer. One rebel officer stood on the parapet and rallied his soldiers to hold the line. "Hurray, my brave men," the Southern commander yelled in encouragement. James Gardiner of the 36th spotted him and was overcome with fury. He rushed in advance of his brigade, leaving himself unshielded and unprotected, and shot the Confederate commander. The wounded officer still stood as Gardiner continued to charge toward him with bayonet pointed. Gardiner drove his bayonet so deep into the rebel officer that the gun's muzzle entered the man. The rebel soldiers quickly lost their will to defend the works.

Edward Ratcliff, a first sergeant from Yorktown, Virginia, was the first enlisted man to enter the enemy works. His company commander had been killed in the charge. Ratcliff led the men of the 38th, Company C, forward and stormed the fortifications. Private William H. Barnes, from the same company, showed equal courage. He was wounded during the advance but, undeterred, was among the first to breach the rebel barricades. Sergeant James Harris of the 38th also was among the heroes that day, valiantly charging the enemy fortifications.

Scroggs, the white officer leading a division of the 5th, watched as the black troops "pressed forward bravely following their colors. . . . The Color bearer was killed on one side of me and my orderly [sergeant] wounded on the other, two of my [sergeants] killed and my company seemingly annihilated, yet on we went through the double line of abatis, and over their works like a whirlwind."

He saw the courage of black soldiers all around him. He was especially moved by one of his own men. "My O.S. Wm. Strander scarce 20 years of age and as brave a boy as ever wore the diamond refused to go to the rear on being wounded: but with the blood streaming from his neck followed me over the enemy's works."

The black soldiers poured over the parapet in an unrelenting wave. The famed Texas regiments fled so quickly that the Union soldiers could take but a few prisoners. The rebels gathered in the woods on the side of Signal Hill, but Draper's troops charged, forcing them to again flee. Draper's brigade, which had started out with 1,300 men, lost almost 450. Of thirty-two line officers, eleven had fallen.

Jubilant over the breakthrough, Butler quickly messaged Grant at 8:30 A.M. An hour later, the lieutenant general received the note telling him that along with the success of the black troops, Ord's first column had smashed the enemy's line of defense and had captured Fort Harrison. The success of the black troops had prevented the Confederates from sending reinforcements to the fort. Kautz's Union cavalry had followed the black troops and were now heading toward Richmond.

"Birney has advanced from Deep Bottom and taken the main line of works at the signal tower, New Market Heights, which commands the road, and is advancing," Butler wrote. Butler singled out the black troops for praise, saying, "Paine's division took their line handsomely, with considerable loss."

The commander of the James rode over the battlefield to

view the fallen troops. He took great care as he moved among the bodies. He had witnessed the brave, glorious charge and considered hallowed the ground on which the dead lay. Years later, he would recall in vivid detail the bravery and uncommon valor of the men who took New Market Heights.

The black troops paused for about half an hour after the morning assault. Ambulances rushed to the battlefield as the survivors gathered their regiments and tried to determine the dead and missing. They looked for bodies in the underbrush. Some of the dead were horribly disfigured by gunfire, others stripped of their clothing by the enemy. Among those killed was Nathaniel Danks, the handsome soldier who had dashed out of ranks to kiss the pretty girl on a porch in Yorktown to the cheers of his fellow soldiers. Big Sam Johnson, a small, slightly built man, nicknamed for his gift at telling big stories, lay dead on the field. He looked as if he had curled up for a nap.

"I couldn't help shedding a few tears when I realized that he was indeed dead," noted a saddened McMurray. "And even now when I think of him I feel a pang of sorrow that his cheerful light of life was extinguished so early. He was probably just 25 years old. I looked at him a few moments, said 'goodbye, Sam,' and was compelled to go on without seeing that he was decently buried."

There was no time to mourn.

The dead were left in the field where they fell. With the rebels on the run, the black troops now turned their attention to the Confederate capital. The cry "On to Richmond" rippled through their ranks. But the men who marched toward Richmond were indescribably changed from a few hours earlier. They had succeeded where others failed and captured a seemingly impenetrable fortress on a hill long coveted by Union generals. Victory came at a high price for these warriors. But the scale that measures human endeavor was tipped in their favor.

For on this day, the black soldiers had charged the gates of hell and come away victors.

Once again, Richmond, which had stubbornly resisted capture, was at the epicenter of the war. The city was of such vital importance to both sides that Grant and Lee rode out to the battle site to personally direct operations. As the Union's top general approached the line at the crossroads between New Market and Mill roads near Signal Hill, he came within view of the black troops. The men, still on an adrenaline high from the morning's battle, cheered the commander as he and his staff rode by. Grant's presence confirmed the importance of their mission.

"Saw Gen. Grant and staff, both Birneys and other 'stars,'" an obviously pleased Fleetwood wrote in his diary. It was General Birney who had helped convince Fleetwood to join the Union army a little more than a year earlier.

There was a flurry of dispatches between Grant, Lincoln, and top generals all morning. By 10:45 A.M., Grant learned that both columns of Butler's attack had been victorious and telegraphed the good news from Chaffin's Farm back to Washington.

"General Ord's corps advanced this morning and carried the very strong fortifications and long line of [entrenchments] below Chaffin's farm, with some 15 pieces of artillery and from 200 to 300 prisoners. General Ord was wounded in the leg, though not dangerously. General Birney advanced at the same time from Deep Bottom, and carried the New Market road and [entrenchments] and scattered the enemy in every direction, though he captured but few. He is now pushing on toward Richmond."

General Lee, realizing the serious peril Richmond faced, was rushing thousands of troops to defend the Southern capital. At least sixteen train carloads of gray-clad troops from Petersburg were heading toward the city. In addition, Union intelligence reports showed a column of about two thousand Confederate troops heading to the city along the Richmond turnpike. Another four thousand men were on the move near Petersburg.

Grant passed the information on the movement of Confederate troops to Butler with the admonition, "You will see that all must be done today that can be done toward Richmond." He was only too painfully aware that past indecisions by Butler and others had doomed previous attempts to capture Richmond and Petersburg.

President Lincoln was encouraged by the success of the black troops as well as Ord's capture of Fort Harrison. But he telegraphed his concerns to Grant about the vulnerability of Sheridan if Lee chose to send troops to help Early.

Grant promised that the assault on Richmond would prevent that by forcing the Confederates to concentrate their efforts on defending the city. Even now, he pointed out, his men were closing in on the city: "Our advance is now within six miles of Richmond and [has] captured some very strong enclosed forts."

The exhausted black troops pressed toward Richmond in the midday heat. Three miles into the march, they came upon an uncompleted line of rebel defenses that had been deserted. These defenses, just three miles from Richmond, were the last obstacles between Union troops and the city.

As most of Birney's force marched toward the city, the 5th Colored Regiment and 118th New York Infantry were a mile away approaching Fort Gilmer and Laurel Hill. Almost immediately, they came under intense rebel artillery fire. The first wave of fire proved deadly. "A spherical Case ricocheted a few feet from where I was at the time standing and struck a soldier a few rods in rear of me severing his right leg from his body," Scroggs said.

The troops took cover in the nearby trees and quickly reorganized. Moving through the dense undergrowth for about a mile, they emerged with a clear view of the enemy fortifications. Almost immediately, the order came to storm the enemy defenses.

From where the Union soldiers stood, it was difficult to judge the terrain between them and the rebels. But once again, they could see daunting obstacles: three sharp ravines, fallen trees, waterlogged marshland, and a well-entrenched, heavily armed rebel force. Increasing the danger exponentially, one of the rebel batteries was positioned to shell the entire length of the ravines. At no time during the charge would the men be free from enemy fire.

The plan of attack was explained. The 118th New York would lead the assault, with the black troops providing support. The troops were ordered to lie down for a few moments to catch their breath before making the charge. But even on the ground, they were exposed to rebel fire.

When the order to charge was given, the men raced forward. They were met with withering fire and some soldiers of the 118th, disoriented and bloody, fell back and sought shelter in a nearby house. The black troops rushed passed the white regiment, forming the new front line of the assault.

The swampy ground slowed their advance as intense rebel fire thinned their ranks. Men fell by the dozens. Pinn, who had been heroic in the morning charge, was wounded. The Confederates unleashed the heaviest fire at the third ravine. "We finally struggled through the last swamp and up the last bank, to find ourselves alone and unsupported, exposed to an enfilading fire of artillery and musketry in front which now for the first began to tell upon our ranks with murderous effect," Scroggs recalled.

The men pressed forward through what Scroggs described as

"pitiless hail of lead and iron. On, on, with a blind desperation: seeming to have but one idea in view, one purpose, one end to accomplish, and that, to die an honorable death."

Some of the soldiers appeared oblivious to the danger, charging into what seemed certain death. They came within a hundred yards of the works when it became evident that pressing further was impossible and would mean the total annihilation of the regiment. Scroggs later recalled the desperate charge.

"I seen a man of my own Co. [Fleming Taylor] get up, step out a dozen yards in front of the line and coolly fire his piece at the enemy, then slowly follow the Co. from the ground. I seen a Sergeant who had received three different wounds crying because the battalion would not go farther. I seen men tenderly and slowly carrying their wounded captain [Wilber] off that field of death, and also their wounded comrades, from where to delay was almost madness. I seen all this and more, and no man dare hereafter say aught in my presence against the bravery and soldierly qualities of the colored soldiers."

Those who did not leave the field were captured. Men almost too exhausted to walk urged themselves to keep moving out of fear of being taken prisoner. Scroggs's company was reduced to ten men from the fifty that began the march that day. He was taken by ambulance back to the Union line in a state of delirium. "So closed that day, a parallel to which I never wish to experience," he wrote.

One Confederate soldier described the battle as "a most violent assault on Fort Gilmer. Many negroes were killed in the ditch." General Robert E. Lee arrived on the scene to inspire his troops.

Duncan's brigade watched the charge in the distance. McMurray described the scene: "We saw these black men pass the white troops, go on until they reached the ditch, jump into the ditch, and attempt to climb up the face of the parapet into the fort, and saw some of them clubbed down with rebel muskets."

It was a costly repulse for the Union. Draper's brigade, which had lost 447 men at New Market Heights, lost another 106 soldiers at Fort Gilmer.

Lee's reinforcements prevented any further advance by Butler's army. The high hopes for capturing Richmond vanished. By late afternoon, the secondary goal of the mission now became the primary focus. Grant's dispatch to Halleck in Washington explained this. "I did not expect to carry Richmond, but was in hopes of causing the enemy so to weaken the garrison of Petersburg as to be able to carry that place. The great object, however, is to prevent the enemy sending reinforcements to Early," who was locked in battle with Sheridan in the Shenandoah Valley.

Grant worried that the Union soldiers could be trapped at nightfall between the city, the James River, and the advancing rebel troops. He advised Butler to choose a safe spot for the night and attack again in the morning if the rebels declined to send no more than a division to protect the city.

But the rebels had no intention of giving up Richmond and sent in thousands of troops. As the Confederate soldiers flooded into the embattled city, they set their sights on retaking Fort Harrison, captured by Union forces earlier in the day.

The rebels lined up to charge the fort in the late afternoon. Because of Draper's wounds, his black troops, now being led by Colonel Ames, prepared up to repulse the attack. The tables were turned. The Union soldiers were now safely entrenched and the Confederates would have to brave the hazards and enemy fire to charge the fortifications. Fleetwood, Veal, Hawkins, and Kelly remembered the brutal enemy gunfire that had decimated their ranks earlier in the day and now honed their sights to exact some measure of revenge.

The Confederates formed a charging column in a grove of oak trees near the defenses captured by black troops earlier. The gathering mass of gray gave the Union troops a clear indication as to where the rebels would focus their attack, allowing the men to prepare for the advance. The black troops crouched behind the fortifications, which were between three and four feet high and built of logs with earth thrown against them.

At the point where the heaviest attack was expected, Brigadier General George J. Stannard's Vermont division was positioned, armed with Spencer repeating rifles that held seven bullets that could be fired before the need to reload. Behind them stood a second line equipped with ordinary army rifles. The black troops, armed with their standard single-shot muskets, were positioned to provide flanking fire at the point where the rebels were expected to try to break the Union line.

The Southern army opened on the Union line with forty guns of deafening cannon fire. Fleetwood, Veal, Hawkins, and Kelly moved into position and waited for the rebels to appear.

Amid the shells, Union commanders continued to try to rush regiments into place. The danger was demonstrated when a Union soldier scampering to get in place was struck by an enemy shell, sending all his belongings flying.

As the men waited for the Confederate charge, they could see a staff officer from another regiment crouching behind the breastwork as shells exploded around him. This infuriated Colonel Ames, the man leading Fleetwood's brigade in place of the wounded Duncan. Ames swore at the officer, calling him a coward and demanding that he walk upright like a man. To emphasize the point, Ames jumped on the breastworks oblivious to the shells flying overhead and walked back and forth the length of his regiment two or three times. His display of courage had the desired effect. At that moment, every man in the regiment would have followed the audacious Ames into the most severe enemy fire.

Within minutes, the artillery fire slackened—an unmistakable sign the charge was about to begin. On cue, the Confederates emerged from the grove of oak trees, rushing forward with an aura of invincibility. At first, the rebels came on without uttering a word. The Union troops held their fire, waiting patiently until they drew closer. Then the gray advancing tide unleashed the unnerving rebel yell and charged at a pace close to a full run. The Federal troops opened fire.

"And such a roar of musketry as followed I never heard before, it seemed to me," McMurray noted. "What with the rebel yell, and the roar of our muskets, and our own shouting, a man might as well have been deaf for a little while."

The Confederates, their ranks thinning by the second, continued the charge despite the hail of Union lead, coming within a few feet of the works before being forced back. The onslaught of Union fire proved too much even for the stoutest heart, and the rebels finally retreated, running at full speed. Fleetwood, Hawkins, Veal, and Kelly joined the shout of victory from the Union ranks. A few of the men leaped over the breastworks and chased the fleeing enemy, who disappeared in the grove of trees.

With Fort Harrison secure, the troops were ordered out of the works to find quarters for the night. The black troops set up tents where Confederate soldiers had slept the previous night. Fleetwood, though exhausted, helped stack arms and then spent a restless night, moving three times and ending up in the darkness of a captured stronghold. As he settled in the captured rebel works, one of the most significant days for black soldiers in U.S. history was coming to a close. It was hard to know this by the succinct summary of the day's events in Fleetwood's diary.

"Coffee boiled and line formed. Moved out and on. Charged with the 6th at daylight and got used up. Saved colors. Remnants of the two gathered and maneuvering under Col. Ames of 6th U.S. Colored Troops. Marched in line and flank all day. Saw Gen. Grant and staff, both Birneys and other 'stars.'"

As the day closed, they were still counting the dead and wounded.

Later, when he had a private moment, Fleetwood carefully tallied the number of fallen comrades in a ledger page at the back of his diary. On the page, provided to record incidental purchases, he noted the dead almost as an accountant would show items on a balance sheet. "Killed," he wrote in the upper left-hand column of the ledger page, "Captain 1, Sergeants 4, Corporals 3, Privates 19." Under the heading to record dollars and cents, he totaled those killed, "27."

He continued down the left-hand side of the page. "Wounded, Captains 1, 1st Lieuts 3, 2nd Lieuts 1, Sergeants 15, Corporals 21, Privates 95." Again he tallied the entries, showing the total number of wounded at 136.

He noted fourteen missing privates. Total losses, September 29, "177," he wrote, noting at the bottom of the page that the regiment began the day with only 11 officers and 305 men. More than half the men in his unit were wounded, missing, or dead.

The cold numbers belied Fleetwood's personal anguish. The dead and wounded included friends and close acquaintances.

Pinn, wounded at Fort Gilmer, was taken to the hospital along with James Harris and William H. Barnes. Miles James's arm was amputated. Alfred B. Hilton, the strapping farmer who saved the colors and rallied his regiment, lost his leg below the knee and lay grievously ill. He would die three weeks later in a hospital at Fort Monroe.

The sacrifices made by black soldiers that day were duly noted. Two weeks later, the names "New Market Heights" and "Petersburg" were inscribed on the regimental flags of the black regiments in official recognition of the bravery shown by the soldiers. But the men who displayed uncommon valor that day didn't need the insignias as reminders. Their characters had been proven in fierce battle, and none would soon forget the wild, glorious charge on that foggy September morning. Yet Fleetwood and the other survivors knew the war was not yet won.

But there was cause for celebration, for those who had questioned whether the black man would fight had gotten their answer. Not only would he fight, but he would beat impossible odds to win.

———∞∞∞———

THE WAR ENDS

Less than seven months after the battle of New Market Heights, the American Civil War, for all intents and purposes, was over. On April 9, 1865, generals Lee and Grant met at Appomattox Court House, a small community amid the rolling hills of rural central Virginia, to formalize the surrender of Lee's army. The war that began with the boom of cannons and heavy artillery at Fort Sumter, South Carolina, ended quietly in a private home that was once a tavern with the signing of a simple two-page document that laid out the terms of surrender.

Three days later, Fleetwood and the members of his regiment got the news as they marched toward Raleigh, North Carolina. They had been part of a massive campaign in that state as the Union troops pushed south. Shouts of joy rippled through the ranks as the news was passed forward. The moment they had all prayed and longed for was finally at hand.

"Everyone was wild with joy and excitement and the cheers and yells of satisfaction made that particular portion of the Old North State echo the sounds of loyalty," said a man in Fleetwood's brigade.

Not all the Southern troops had surrendered, and battles and skirmishes continued. But now it was only a matter of time. Complete victory, once measured in months and years, was days or, at worst, weeks away.

Since their formal inclusion in the war some two years earlier, Fleetwood and his fellow blacks had experienced much. He marveled at the changes sweeping the nation.

When Fleetwood enlisted, slavery was legal in his home state of Maryland and all across the South. Now that dreaded blight on American society was finally ended in his and every state. And importantly, the black man had fought to help end it. Fleetwood and thirteen others who fought at New Market Heights had medals of honor to prove it.

This mild-mannered, bookish shipping clerk was no longer the raw, uncertain recruit who showed up at Camp Birney in the summer of 1863. He'd been shot at and returned fire countless times, repeatedly charging across open fields under murderous enemy fire. He'd won the nation's highest military honor, a prize he cherished for the sake of his race as much as his own reputation.

At the outset of the war, black volunteers had been turned away. Now as the end neared, blacks made up 10 percent of Union forces. Initially, black troops were used only to dig ditches and build fortifications because Union officials had little faith in their ability to fight. But when finally given the chance to wage war, they had proved themselves peerless fighters.

There had been stirring victories. Fleetwood and the other black soldiers helped clear guerrillas from the swamps of North Carolina and shared the glory when City Point was captured and the fortifications near Petersburg and New Market Heights taken. Many men had died in those battles, but their sacrifice proved not to be in vain.

Not all the battles ended in victory, and the black soldiers had their share of bitter defeats. Fleetwood was present at the Petersburg mine fiasco and the ill-fated first expedition to Fort Fisher, at Wilmington, North Carolina. In that expedition, Federal forces tried taking the heavily fortified fort with a combined land and sea assault. Wrangling between top Union officers, bad weather, and a bungled attempt to blow up the fort with a vessel packed with explosives doomed the mission. Union troops avenged that loss months later, and the black soldiers were there when the fort eventually fell during the largest naval bombardment and amphibious landing of the war.

A clerk long accustomed to keeping track of numbers, Fleetwood lost count of the miles he had marched and the number of battlefields and fortifications he had assaulted. With the exception of New Market Heights, he kept no running score of the men he had seen die or the number of friends he had lost. Some things were better not tallied.

Now with the war all but over, Fleetwood's thoughts turned to the future. Despite the great hardships he had encountered as a soldier, he wanted a career in the army. He would later abandon that hope after being denied an officer's commission because of his color. Slavery, Fleetwood would discover, was officially ended, but the racism it bred was still safely ensconced in American society.

But in the heady days of April 1865, the stench of blood, gore, and rotting corpses was already fading. The Union was saved and slavery erased from American society. Former slaves and free blacks could proudly say they played their part, and not too minor or shabby a role.

And in the official military records that chronicle the daring dashes and glorious charges of America's bloody civil war, there would be mention of the events of New Market Heights and the brave black soldiers who fought to take that hill; men who in the moment of greatest danger showed unmatched bravery, uncommon valor.

BIBLIOGRAPHY

This book is rooted in primary sources and eyewitness accounts. Whenever possible, we have allowed the men who fought in the battles depicted in these pages to describe the events in their own words. We relied heavily on *The Official Records of the War of the Rebellion* (Washington, D.C., 1880), published by the U.S. Government Printing Office. Also invaluable were the maps in *The Official Military Atlas of the Civil War*. These maps compiled by the U.S. military aided greatly in tracking the journeys of the regiments involved in this story.

The Christian Fleetwood Papers in the U.S. Library of Congress, including his daily diary and writings about race and the service of blacks in the U.S. military (notably his pamphlet *The Negro as a Soldier* [1895]), provided a rare, deeply personal look at the life of the black soldier during the Civil War. We owe both his military service and his record of it a deep debt.

The service records of the black Medal of Honor winners obtained from the U.S. National Archives helped in tracking the military careers of these soldiers. We also relied on letters detailing events by soldiers such as Milton B. Holland, which have been published in several books, including Joseph B. Mitchell's *The Badge of Gallantry: Letters from Civil War Medal of Honor Winners* (Shippensburg, Pa.: White Mane Books, 1997).

A number of soldiers involved in the incidents in this book also left memoirs that provided a variety of vantage points from which to view these events. Starting from the top of the chain of command on down, we relied on accounts from: *Personal Memoirs of U.S. Grant/Selected Letters, 1839–1865* (New York: Library of America, 1990); *Butler's Book* by Benjamin F. Butler (Boston: A. M. Thayer & Co., 1892); *Autobiography of Maj. Gen. William F. Smith* (Dayton, Ohio: Morningside House Inc., 1990); *Autobiography of Isaac Jones Wistar, 1827–1905: Half a Century in War and Peace* (Philadelphia: Wistar Institute of Anatomy and Biology, 1937); *Recollections of a Colored Troop* by John McMurray, Major, 6th U.S.C.T. (Brookville, Pa.: McMurray Co., 1916; reprinted 1994); and *J. J. Scroggs' Diary and Letters, 1852–1865*, compiled by Larry Leigh (Thomaston, Ga., 1996).

We also consulted hundreds of Civil War–era pamphlets concerning black soldiers, civil rights, black history, and accounts of actions by the regiments of the Medal of Honor winners. Newspapers, magazines, and books from the period also yielded critical information. In particular, we quoted or drew from the following newspapers and periodicals: C. C. Hazewell, "The Beginning of the End," *Atlantic Monthly* 13, no. 75 (January 1864): 112–123; Theophilus J. Minton, "Robert Brown Elliott," *African Methodist Episcopal Church Review* (1892); *Douglass' Monthly* V (August 1863): 852; the *Detroit News*, January 7, 1874; the *New York Herald*, April 16, 1864; the *New York Times*, July 7, 1863; July 15,

1863; and January 6, 1874; the *Southern Illustrated News* (Richmond, Va.), April 30, 1864. We also drew from a biographical sketch of Christian Fleetwood by Charles Johnson Jr. on the National Park Service's Richmond National Battlefield Web site, "Fleetwood Biography," www.nps.gov/rich/flee~172.htm.

Three books published in the fifty or so years after the end of the war proved useful to our research: Frederick H. Dyer, *A Compendium of the War of the Rebellion* (3 vols.; Des Moines, 1908); William F. Fox, *Regimental Losses in the American Civil War* (Albany, N.Y., 1889); and George J. Williams, *History of the Negro Troops, 1861–1865* (New York, 1888).

Finally, we include several books that were not only invaluable to us but might provide interested readers with more insight into both the Civil War and the role of black troops in it: Mark M. Boatner, *The Civil War Dictionary* (New York: D. McKay Co., 1959); Paddy Griffith, *Battle in the Civil War* (New Haven: Yale University Press, 1986); E. B. Long with Barbara Long, *The Civil War Day by Day: An Almanac 1861–1865* (Garden City, N.Y.: Doubleday, 1971); James M. McPherson, *Battle Cry of Freedom: The Civil War Era* (New York: Oxford University Press, 1988) and *The Negro's Civil War: How American Blacks Felt and Acted During the War for the Union* (New York: Pantheon Books, 1965); James M. Paradis, *Strike the Blow for Freedom: The 6th United States Colored Infantry in the Civil War* (Shippensburg, Pa.: White Mane Books, 1998); Carl Sandburg, *Abraham Lincoln* (4 vols.; New York: Harcourt, Brace, 1954); Noah Andre Trudeau, *Like Men of War: Black Troops in the Civil War* (Boston: Little, Brown, 1998); Geoffrey C. Ward with Ric Burns and Ken Burns, *The Civil War* (New York: Vintage, 2000); and Versalle F. Washington, *Eagles on Their Buttons: A Black Infantry Regiment in the Civil War* (Columbia: University of Missouri Press, 1962); Shelby Foote, *The Civil War, a Narrative* (New York: Random House, 1974).

INDEX